Going Deeper

Insight Toward Intimacy in Christ

David A. Case

GOING DEEPER
Copyright © 1998 by Live Free Ministries
1064 14th Ave., McPherson, KS 67460
(316)-241-8911

Library of Congress Catalog Card Number: 99-94219
ISBN 0-9662598-0-7

Acknowledgements

I would like to thank the many people that have encouraged me to press on in the things that I am learning and teaching. First and foremost would be my wife, Kelly, whose unconditional love and acceptance has given me the confidence to face each new step of growth in Christ without fear, as I always know that she will be there to back me. I also want to thank my children, Amy, Derek, and Seth, who have been a real joy to be around, and have honored me, encouraged me, and been patient with me in the long hours of work.

My church family certainly has been a key to drawing out some of the principles that you will read in this book. They are a group of people that are hungry for God and have been willing to endure some of the tests that a deeper walk can bring. They have continually challenged me to lead them into more truth, and I thank God for their support.

This book probably would not exist if it had not been for a few key individuals that helped me focus on the idea of publishing. Evangelist Paul Conger may have been the first and most consistent voice telling me I needed "to get it in a book." Rev. James Lilley, Janet Roesti, Jim and Cindy Cooprider, Rhonda Treder, Rev. Jason Pickering, and Rick Thompson are a few of the many others that also stepped up at key times to say "You can and should press on with this book and this ministry!" Without the encouragement of these and many others (and certainly the Lord's nudging), I would most likely have limited my vision to impacting a church.

I also want to thank God for my parents for the training I received during my growing up years. They taught me to work hard and to take appropriate risks, both of which were vital to my going forward in this venture. They helped lay the foundations and to establish in me the persistence that is needed to go deeper in Christ.

I would love to name many others who have been personal friends, staff members, mentors, editors to the book, ministry supporters, and givers of insight. Many people have made significant contributions to my growth, which I in turn try to relate to you in this book. God has mentored me through many and He above all is to be praised and thanked. To Him be all glory and honor and praise!

TABLE OF CONTENTS

Introduction

I know of very few Christians who do not want to grow deeper in Christ. I know of many who have given up the thought of ever overcoming the "sin which so easily ensnares us" (Hebrews 12:1b). For them, the challenges to growth are no longer an encouragement, but a thorn, and a reminder of the feelings of helplessness that accompany not being able to do the simple things that Christ calls us to do.

This book is about restoring hope in overcoming those things that keep us from Going Deeper in Christ. If all things are normal, growth is a given. Little babies do not have to ask their parents permission to grow. In fact, if growth does not occur, we take them to the doctor to find out what is wrong. So it is spiritually! Growth is a given. If growth is not occurring, we need to take it to the Word of God and to prayer to see what is blocking the growth.

There are times when medical treatment is very costly. Often, finding the exact cause is a long and difficult process. Yet, the right doctor, with the right tests, can quickly and easily identify physical problems with which he is familiar. So it is with our Doctor, Jesus Christ. Having walked the human walk, He can quickly identify our difficulties and intercede until there is a solution. Our need is to go to the Doctor and to follow the cures that He prescribes.

Growth in Christ is normal– at least it should be. Although, the principles in this book are not so difficult to understand, they can be difficult to apply. The understanding is most often the easy part. The doing is usually the hard part.

Often, physical cures are not difficult to understand. Yet frequently, the doctor's orders are simply not carried out. Many a doctor has lamented with great frustration over a patient that could have been well if only he or she had followed instructions.

So it is with spiritual growth. We have the perfect manual for growth. We have the perfect Doctor. We have all we need if only we will believe and obey. Often it is the most simple steps that are lacking. It is my hope that these pages are written in such a way that it will make it a little easier for you to follow through in obedience to Christ to new levels of growth and victory. I hope and pray that through these pages, you will begin to experience the exhilaration of Going Deeper in Christ.

Finally, I believe that most of the readers of a book with this title are interested in growing spiritually. I have chosen to write much of the book in the first person (I or we) deliberately because of our common struggle to walk in a manner that is worthy of the calling of Christ. May we enter into this experience as fellow learners of the ways of His life.

Chapter One

"Busted"

As my wife and I were driving down the highway, a question emerged from my lips almost without warning. "Kelly, who do you think I am more like: my mom or my dad?" We were on our way back from a Christian seminar at the time, and I was mulling over the log and the speck principle from Matthew seven. "Your mom," came the reply from my wife as she continued to casually guide the wheel of the car, gazing straight ahead.

That simple answer rocked my world. Though I don't remember "the issues," I do remember that I was frustrated with my mom. She had challenged me in some areas that I didn't want to be challenged. I was an adult now! I was married! And I was in no mood to be receiving advice, especially advice that went against my own way of thinking.

In asking my wife the question, some of those frustrations were on my mind, and I wasn't ready for my wife's answer. In my mind, my mother had been too aggressive with me. She had stepped over the line of her authority. My picture of reality painted me as being more laid back, more like my dad who in this situation had not had much to say. My ego was busy telling me that I would not make the same "mistake" that my mother had made.

With a response that was too easy, too automatic, my wife turned the focus of my thoughts from my mother, back to me. The log and the speck principle was now reality. My mother had a speck, and I had the log. I started to tell the joke only to find that the joke was on me.

My first reaction was a strong urge to verbally dissect my wife's answer. The smooth flow of my thoughts had been thrown into a skid and brought to a not-so-smooth stop. Could it really be true? Was my wife really right? Was I really more like my mom? And if this was true, what else was true about me that I didn't even have the slightest clue about?

During my years as a school teacher, it had been a part of my job to spot the hidden things and expose them. I would always try to be quiet about discipline, not wanting to embarrass anyone. On one occasion, I can remember spotting something sinister going on in a corner of the class. In a very casual way, I stood and slowly began to make my way over toward the prime suspect, thinking that I was not calling any particular attention to the situation. When I was just a few feet from the student, a not-so-quiet "Busted!" cry echoed gleefully across the room.

"Busted!" This time my wife was the teacher and I was the student. I was the one being exposed. At a moment when I least suspected it, my image of myself had been rendered unreliable. My neat packages of "perfect understanding" were judged as wanting. Suddenly I felt very vulnerable. If, on such a simple matter as this, I was wrong, where else was I totally off base?

The conference that I had attended had taught me about the truths of the log and speck principle of Matthew seven. The lecturer had illustrated that we tend to be most frustrated with and critical of people who are the most like us, since they mirror our own shortcomings. We generally do not like to see our own weaknesses in graphic detail, a detail that is often seen when a child looks at parent or sometimes when a parent looks at a child. The conference had also shown me that our frustration is often greatly out of proportion with the truth. The one with the "log" is critical of the one with the "speck."

I understood all of this and was very adept at applying it to my wife, or my mother, or anyone else for that matter. The conference had revealed truth *to* me. My wife had revealed truth *in* me. Everything in me cried, "Foul!" I had wanted reassurance of my own goodness and of the new understanding I had gained about life. My ego did not want to accept that its way of thinking was wrong. Praise God! I resisted the urge to answer back.

Part of what was happening to me (and in me) was just a normal growth pattern. Teenagers often distance themselves from their parents and even develop a critical attitude toward their parents as a part of the process of establishing independence. As the years go by, generally both the distance and the critical thought patterns tend to be erased.

Looking back, I know that my reaction was greatly out of proportion to reality. Even though I was no longer a teenager, I was still trying to establish my independence. I was unsure whether or not I really was right, partially because of my mother's challenge, and I was trying to reassure myself . . . at the expense of my mother.

In the process, I had taken offense toward one that I dearly loved and respected. That is not uncommon. The greatest offenses are generally toward those you love the most, especially parents. With the greater love comes the greater potential for hurt.

I am very grateful to my parents, especially my mom, for a Godly heritage. Even at that time, I'm sure that I knew that fact and could have recited my gratefulness to anyone who asked. But my reaction was not a reaction of logic that surveyed all factors and then gave an appropriate response. It was a reaction of one desperately searching for a vindication of self despite the information just received. It was a typical reaction of the ego to truth.

Yet, in this incident, it was not just my relationship with my parents that was in question but my relationship with God. When truth came, I had to make a choice. I could either accept the truth or reject it. If I chose to accept the truth about myself and humble myself before God, I would end up closer to Him. If I chose to reject the truth, a spiritual wall would be erected between me and God.

When truth comes via an offense, we can accept it or reject it. If the person is one we love, we have a tendency to try to bury the incident thinking that honesty about the weaknesses of a loved one is a kind of hatred. The irony is that facing truth in an open and honest way will, in most cases, actually draw us closer to the very one that has offended us.

Why? Because in most cases, God is revealing truth to us and about us through the offense. The offense serves as a mirror of self, and we don't like what we see. Typically we turn the focus toward the other person and blind ourselves to self, or we try to bury the whole incident and block truth totally.

When we react God's way and receive the truth, we focus more on self than on the offender. Having seen the truth of our own weakness, the weakness of the offender suddenly takes on a whole new perspective. Instead of hating the offender, a compassion develops for one that is struggling in a similar area.

Especially with loved ones, it is good to get an accurate picture of the truth, weaknesses and all.

If we are not careful, we reject the truth or bury the truth. Bitterness sets in and what begins as an offense toward man, ends as an offense toward God. Why? Because unresolved offenses make for an awful life. And sooner or later, an awful life will result in a hatred toward God.

Facing the truth about self, especially at the time of an offense, seems like a minor issue compared to the "important" things of life. Yet this one thing often ends up being the battle line between spiritual life and spiritual death. In order to draw closer both to loved ones and to God, we must be willing to change our view of ourselves. We must embrace truth in the inner man.

Limitations of Logic

In the Western world, we have been well trained in logic and in scientific principles. Knowledge is an idea that we learn in a book. We attend conferences or classes to store up more content of something that we call knowledge. It is an idea that we can express and put to some sort of practical test. It is, in the end, almost impersonal and factual much like the law of gravity.

The Biblical notion of knowledge is very different. In the gospel of John, Jesus tells us that "You shall know the truth, and the truth shall make you free." Knowledge of the truth has a very personal and practical impact. It is not something to be stored up, processed, and then regurgitated much the way a computer would do. In this Scripture, the end result of knowing the truth is the very practical promise of personal freedom. Head knowledge alone does not measure up to the standard of Biblical knowledge of the truth.

Paul writes in 1 Corinthians 13:1 that "Though I have the gift of prophecy, and understand all mysteries and all knowledge, and though I have all faith, so that I could remove mountains, but have not love, I am nothing." Knowledge of the future and even of "all mysteries" is declared of no value unless it has the stamp of love. Biblical knowledge is meant to result in a change toward a personal godliness. Knowledge without love is not true knowledge.

Factual knowledge is just a body of information. It is understanding the log and speck principle and being able to repeat back the basic content of the idea. Real knowledge produces an eternal result: "This is eternal life, that they may know You, the only true God, and Jesus Christ whom You have sent" (John 17:3). Real knowledge, according to the Scriptures, brings a real change. The person that "knows" Christ "is" in eternal life. He doesn't know about eternal life; he **has** eternal life. The Pharisees were often described as handling the words of God but not having the Word of God in them.

Real knowledge changes us. Knowing God is not knowing about God. Knowing God is an encounter that will forever change our being. For some, a brief encounter with God causes them to run fast and hard in the opposite direction. Others open up their hearts to God and are radically changed into that image of love that is of eternal value.

I knew about the log and speck principle before I left the conference. I began to know the log and speck principle as the result of a simple answer by my wife. Knowledge of the log and speck principle was no longer factual and distant. It was no longer for the other person. It was the truth of God being revealed to me, that I was not the person that I thought I was. And neither was my mother. A minor frustration had caused me to create an image of life that was not true. I needed to know the truth, God's truth, *in* me.

The Role of Truth

Going deeper with God is to know God more intimately. It is also to know myself better. That is where most people lose it. To understand more of God's truth, I must understand more of the truth about myself. Truth must be applied to me! When my own depravity begins to surface, often the desire to know God more intimately begins to fade, and it is replaced with a desire to know more *about* God. Though deadly, the change is so subtle that we often don't even notice the difference.

Day by day, it is God's desire to open up a little more of Himself to us, in us, and through us. He wants us to know Him, The Truth, in a much greater way. Unfortunately, that God kind of knowledge requires our life. We can't just know about truth, but we must live the truth to know the truth. We must begin to "walk a mile in God's shoes" in order to fully know Him. We must be willing to change and to become like Him to fully know Him. We must lose our lives to get His life!

It is His desire to eventually transform us into a perfect picture of the image of His love, which is a perfect knowledge of Christ. John validates this concept of knowledge: "He who does not love does not know God, for God is love" (1 John 4:8). Much of what we are living now is not in the image of love and thus is not in the image of God. It lacks in the knowledge of God.

Coming home from the conference, I thought that I understood God and had a knowledge of His ways. I thought I was projecting the image of Christ and even would have gladly compared myself in the area of frustration to my mother. If it had stopped there, I would have lacked in the knowledge of God and I certainly had not shown the love of God for my mother.

God's remedy was a wakeup call, compliments of my wife. It was a wakeup call that we call the truth. I had believed a lie about the way life really was. I had flattered myself at the expense of another and, to some extent, at the expense of God. The image of love was not in me which means that the knowledge of God was, at best, hindered. Going deeper with God was out of the question, unless, of course, I allowed the truth to do its work by coming to set me free.

Often our lives make statements like, "God really cannot be trusted to provide my needs" or "I really cannot be expected to do all the things God asks me to do." God wants us to know and live the truth. We are to walk out His love and His life. As we do, our knowledge of Him will increase. Instead, we often declare the situation hopeless and shrink back. We act as if God does not love us, and that the requirement of love is beyond us.

"Let God be true but every man a liar!" (Rom. 3:4b). Because of our fallen nature, we really do express with our lives many things that are not truth. We come to know and live a lie more than we know and live God's truth. It is God's goal for our lives to become a perfect expression of the truth of His love, just as the life of Jesus was and is a perfect expression of the truth of His love. For that to happen, area after area of our lives must be transformed into the image of Jesus Christ. God must confront, with truth, any area of our life that is not like Him.

That all sounds easy enough . . . until the first truth comes our way. Typically we react just as I reacted there in the car. I wanted to hit someone, or yell, or scream. I wanted to run away, or declare it a lie, or at least argue with it. But it hit fast and hard and I knew it was truth. It sank down deep into my being and initially felt like a heavy weight sitting in the pit of my stomach. And that is truth? And that is my reaction to truth?

The Ego Vs. the Truth

Unfortunately, the answer is "Yes!" One of the continuing effects of the fall is that we are inordinately selfish . . . or to put it in more modern terms . . . egoistic. Our whole being now revolves around self and the protection of self. Understanding this fact, advertisers in the modern world tell us that we "deserve" the best and promise us total indulgence. Even churches cater to the selfish man, trying to win salvations with promises of rewards, while leaving out the "death to self" that is also required.

Anything that pumps up the ego tends to feel good . . . unless of course it is excessive, and then even we can recognize that it probably is not true. But those gentle strokes applied in acceptable doses are so effective and powerful in moving people toward a desired end. Why? Because we are still inordinately self-centered.

One of the basic needs of man is that "I want to feel good about me." It is amazing some of the judgments, rationalizations, criticisms, and comparisons that go through our head mainly for just this one purpose: to help make us feel better about ourselves.

By comparison, truth is devastating. It rocks our selfish world. Even the godliest of men, Job and Isaiah, were totally shocked when God pulled back the curtain and showed them Himself. Both had the same reaction: "I am a sinner." Why did they react this way? Did God show them some terrible thing about themselves? NO! He simply showed them a part of Himself. Having seen real truth, they recognized the lies within themselves. These two godly men fell on their faces in repentance.

Jesus said that to receive Him, we would have to die to self. Paul elaborates on that, saying, "I die daily" (1 Cor. 15:31b). The first time truth really hits home, it usually hits. It doesn't touch. It doesn't kiss. It hits. It feels like a real death, a daily death. That is part of why the coward's final destination will be the lake of fire (Rev. 21:8). No coward will face the impact of truth on self. It is far easier on the ego to make excuses, to lie, and even to face devastating consequences than to face the truth. Facing truth is THE test of the kingdom. And the ultimate truth is Jesus, love in pure form. When we see Him as He really is, we will either repent or run.

How is a man born again? The process begins with a recognition of truth about self in the inner man. For it to continue, there must be repentance, but repentance is not enough. There must also be a recognition of the inability to do anything about the selfishness that has been revealed. Otherwise, the person will simply try to fix himself, which is an exercise in futility. Salvation is completed by accepting the remedy that Jesus Christ offers. None of these steps is easy on the ego.

Just the Beginning!

Accepting Jesus is but the beginning of truth in a person's life. It is the first step. There are many steps to go. Even Isaiah and Job, who had already taken many steps toward the truth, were shocked by a clear revelation of the truth. If that is true for two very righteous men, what would an absolute revelation of truth do to you or to me?

We are not equipped to handle it. We would likely become suicidal or deeply depressed or have some other severe reaction. Our ego is too fragile to take it. So God speaks to us a little at a time— one step here and one step there. We say we want total revelation and understanding, but we do not know what we ask. "Busted!" Just one little revelation rocked my world. Thank God! I didn't reject it. Even better, I have come to recognize the reaction of the ego to truth, and, instead of running, I am learning to embrace truth.

Do you really want to grow deep in the Lord? You need truth in the inner man. For those that will take the challenge, the sweetness of the voice and presence of God await you. Those that receive His discipline, receive His love (Prov. 1:20-33). Having seen the pathway, are you ready for more of God?

For the wrath of God is revealed from heaven against all ungodliness and unrighteousness of men, who suppress the truth in unrighteousness, because what may be known of God is manifest in them, for God has shown it to them. For since the creation of the world His invisible attributes are clearly seen, being understood by the things that are made, even His eternal power and Godhead, so that they are without excuse, because, although they knew God, they did not glorify Him as God, nor were thankful, but became futile in their thoughts, and their foolish hearts were darkened.

Romans 1:18-21

Chapter Two

The Light Switch

Over the years, I have struggled with the meaning of this passage in Romans. It is a passage that we often use to answer the question, "How can God condemn the person that has never heard the gospel?"

The answer from verse 19 is that "God has shown it to them."

Yet, I believe that there is an even deeper answer to this question. The wrath of God is revealed against men because they "suppress the truth in unrighteousness." What does that mean? The next phrase at least partially answers the question: " . . . what may be known of God is manifest in them."

The word manifest means brought to light or made visible. "What may be known of God" is made visible to the world by each and every one of us. However, "what may be known of God" is suppressed or hidden when we walk in "unrighteousness." Truth is suppressed by unrighteousness.

Our Number One Job!

God has created each and every one of us with a job to do: to be
a visible representation of His invisible attributes. We are the
light switch. When in the "On" position, we show forth His
beautiful nature of love and goodness. When in the "Off"
position, we demonstrate the grotesqueness of a life without
Christ. If godly, we visibly demonstrate what God is like. If
ungodly, we illustrate God's incredible love for the one that is
ugly, as well as His justice on the day of judgment to come.

Our primary job is to give an understanding of Him to the
universe. In Ephesians 3:10, Paul writes that it is the church that
will make known, or visibly demonstrate, the wisdom of God to
the "principalities and powers in the heavenly places."

It is not just the godless man that needs to see the love of God
expressed. The angels and every creature of the universe is
watching the drama that is unfolding between God and man.
Certainly, through the redemption that was accomplished on the
cross, it is not hard to see that God's love expressed toward
mankind is the ultimate display of love. Jesus, Himself, said,
"Greater love has no one than this, than to lay down one's life
for his friends" (John 15:13).

Through the ages, God has demonstrated His love to man and to
the angels, beginning with Adam. Instead of judging Adam as
He had the angels, God wanted to demonstrate the incredible
depth of His love. Thus, right there in the garden, God killed an
animal to form a covenant with Adam, a covenant that would
eventually mean the death of God's only Son, Jesus.

Love took on a new meaning, with an even greater depth that
had never been seen before. God continued to demonstrate His
character through His long suffering and His mercy toward the

nation Israel. His justice and righteousness demanded judgment, but He had taken care of that through His commitment to sacrifice His Son. His mercy and love prevailed.

God's highest will is for each one of us to recognize His great love and mercy and to begin to respond accordingly. Through the power of His Holy Spirit, that He gives us freely, He wants to transform us into that same perfect image of love that He is. He wants us to be able to extend love even in the difficult situations just as He has done. We are to be the visible expression of His love here on earth. We are "to make known" God to the earth.

Man is meant to be the crowning work, the most excellent demonstration of the love of God. Unfortunately, many times the only way we "illustrate" the love of God is by sinning, which gives God the opportunity to demonstrate forgiveness and mercy. Romans 3:5a says it this way, "But if our unrighteousness demonstrates the righteousness of God, what shall we say?"

It is an amazing fact that even through sin, God triumphs by showing forth a more excellent love that reaches out even to the disgustingly sinful. "Where sin abounded, grace abounded much more, so that as sin reigned in death, even so grace might reign through righteousness to eternal life through Jesus Christ our Lord" (Rom. 6:20b-21). In Christ, the penalty for sin was paid in such an infinite manner, that all sin can be outdone by grace. No sin can hide the love of God. Grace simply abounds "much more."

However, it is "through righteousness" that grace abounds. Jesus' righteousness started the work, but for that work to continue to triumph in today's world, there must be a present manifestation of the righteousness of God. There must be a man

or a woman that is willing to let the Spirit move in his or her life
in such a way that the grace of God can actually be seen. The
gospel needs skin. It needs a human body to be clearly seen by
the world.

An invisible God needs visible flesh to demonstrate the love of
God to a sinful human population. To put it another way, there
must be an intercessor. There must be at least one agent for
God to work through. In Ezekiel 22:30, God reveals that He
needs one man to "stand in the gap" so that judgment might be
averted. Not even Abraham dared ask for a city to be spared for
the sake of one righteous man, but God reveals His heart of
mercy and love.

When there is no intercessor, when the flame of righteousness
has been extinguished or is at least so hidden that it no longer
shows forth His grace, sin comes to the forefront. Grace no
longer restrains the downward spiral. Sin abounds and the earth
becomes more and more grotesque and devoid of the mercy and
love of God that He desires to show forth.

Eventually, judgment must come. If God's love and mercy is to
be seen once again on the earth, the darkness must be stopped.
Love and mercy must come to an end. Judgment must fall so
that the very love of God can be seen once again. As the last
part of Revelation 11:18 puts it, God must "destroy those who
destroy the earth."

Whether through judgment or through mercy, God makes sure
that the earth is seeing a manifestation of His presence on the
earth. He is holy and righteous. If that cannot be demonstrated
through godly men, it can be demonstrated through judgment. It
is not His first choice. He has no pleasure in the death of the
wicked (Ezekiel 18:23). But His glory and life will be
demonstrated on the earth one way or the other: through the

lives of godly men or through the judgment of ungodly men. Even in judgment, it is God's goal to manifest the fullness of His life.

Choosing the Love Manifestation

It is our choice! Do we choose to glorify Him through being transformed into His image of love or by being objects of His wrath (Romans 9:22-24)? Will we choose to display the character of God day by day? Or will we live selfishly, as we are inclined to do?

Projecting an image of His love is the goal for each one of us. It is a visualization of the invisible God that created us. When people see us, the light switch should be "On" and they should think, "Now I better understand what God is like." We should be the love, peace, and joy of God in a very tangible form for the world to see.

Anything short of the image of God is a lie which reflects upon the God that created us. It "suppresses the truth." It darkens the light of His truth meant to be made clear to a lost and dying world. If there are those that have not heard or "seen" the gospel, it is not God who is at fault but you and I, and the many generations that have gradually covered the light of His truth manifest in us.

God is at work, day by day, doing His part to make sure that every man is without excuse, that the light of His glory can be seen in every generation. He has done His part to keep the switch "On." It is the sin of man that has "suppressed the truth" almost to the point of turning the light switch "Off."

Demonstrating That God is the Center

How do we shut off the light of God that is in us? Romans 1:21 says, "Because although they knew God, they did not glorify Him as God, nor were thankful, but became futile in their thoughts, and their foolish hearts were darkened." It all begins with worship. We were created to "glorify Him." We were created to be "thankful."

For us to be a manifestation of the truth of God, we must do those things. But mankind chose to do otherwise. The next verse states that, "Professing to be wise, they became fools." A life that should display that God really is the center of the universe and the all sustaining power of everything that exists, suddenly chose to become the center of its own universe and to try to exist by its own power. The lie was born.

From there, the lie simply becomes more and more clearly manifest. Man moves from worshiping creatures to lusting after others of the opposite sex, to burning for people of the same sex. In verses 28 and 29, the Scriptures tell us that the knowledge of God is lost and is replaced with "all unrighteousness, sexual immorality, wickedness, covetousness, maliciousness . . .".

God is our center. He is our sustainer. He is our total reason for living. He is to be absolutely worshiped all the time. Anything less is a lie. Anything less produces a lifestyle that clearly justifies the judgment of God.

And yet, even in judgment is the love of God manifest through the death of Jesus on the cross. God could have completely wiped us out for our sins. Yet, instead, He chose to take the very penalty for our sins upon Himself. We violated Him, and yet He pays the penalty. When we are at our worst, God's love shines the brightest. He loves the unlovable. God perfectly manifests truth and life. Real life. Real love.

In light of what Christ has done for us, how can we be satisfied with anything less than being a perfect manifestation of the love of God?

The answer is simple. We have tried. We have failed. We have tried again. We have failed again, again, and again. Eventually, we cannot even stand to try again. We cannot face another failure. So, we lower the standard until our egos can smile with success.

Repeated failure is just too much for the ego. It can't handle it. It has to compensate somehow or we go into a spiral of depression and self-destruction. God understands that. He knows that we are but "dust." He judges us accordingly, but even more, He has sent His Son and His Spirit to enable us. He has not left us as orphans. He has not left us helpless.

The real problem is still the same as it was in the beginning: are we going to demand to be the center of the operation or will we let God be at the center? Of ourselves we can do nothing. That is a difficult truth. But when we raise the standard back up to the level God intended, it is much easier to see that our attempts at righteousness are "nothing." Apart from Him, our chance of living real truth is absolutely zero.

Often I hear statements that say God will be unjust if this particular "good man" is not in heaven. Good? In Jesus words,

" Why do you call Me good? No one is good but One, that is, God" (Mark 10:18). If we compare the "goodness" of the lives of the men of our society, those who are better than average we could call "good" men and those below average we could call "bad" men. Instead, we could ask, "Who is a perfect reflection of God?" Or "Who is fulfilling his created purpose of showing forth a perfect image of the love of God?"

The man who does good deeds doesn't quite meet the standard. Real goodness brings a praise of God and not of self (Matt. 5:16). It is easy for the "good" man to slide over into "good" works that actually bring glory to self instead of giving glory to God. When that happens, he gets a very real reward for his good works. It is only a subtle shift, but he does his works in such a way that he is praised for his works. In contrast, the godly man openly admits his own weakness apart from God. His good works are not seen as being done by himself, but as being done with the aid of God.

The "good" man actually feeds his own ego, glorying in his own "goodness." Goodness that brings a glory to self and not to God suddenly doesn't look quite so pure any more. The standard of the God who loved even those who crucified Him eclipses all other standards.

God would be absolutely just in any judgment of man. Instead, He paid the penalty and sent His Holy Spirit. Rather than destroying us, He is willing to enable us if we will only once again recognize our absolute need for Him.

How easy it is to trust in the average, comparing ourselves to others instead of to God! Oh the difference if only we would throw out the averages, trust God fully, and let Him work in and through us! It cannot happen as long as there is even a glimmer of hope that we can reach the standard ourselves.

The stakes are high. The entire universe is watching. God has plans for each one of us to be one of His "stars," one of His shining lights that will be a reflection of His love. We are to demonstrate Him to heaven and earth. Will we try to become THE star, or will we take up our role as one that glorifies THE STAR that really makes it happen?

Hope in self destroys worship. Hope in self turns "Off" the light switch of God's light and love. Hope in God opens the flow of His love in and through you. Is your light switch "On"?

Chapter Three

Seeing God's Face

None of us could face absolute truth. Often stated in the Bible is the idea that "No man can look upon the face of God and live." Our vessels are too weakened by sin to tolerate the kind of absolute revelation that God could give us. Our spiritual makeup has been so marred by our self-centeredness that we can no longer be the kind of direct recipients of fellowship that was normal in the Garden of Eden.

During the first several chapters of Genesis, God shows up. Live. In person. He talks with Adam, Cain, Noah, and Abraham. For years, I thought that God just "spoke" to them with some kind of voice out of the invisible realm, but the more I study these Scriptures, the more I believe that God actually showed up. The generations of sin had not yet weakened the vessels of man to a point where God had to veil His presence.

As the years go on, direct appearances become less and less frequent and more and more veiled. Years later, for Christ to come, Philippians 2 shares that He had to set His glory aside and in John 17:5, Jesus' prayer is that He may now return to the glory which He previously had for all eternity. Only on the Mount of Transfiguration was there a temporary show of His glory, and then it was gone.

So how do we reverse the progressive weakening that sin has brought? God begins the process as described by Isaiah: "For precept must be upon precept, precept upon precept, line upon line, line upon line, here a little, there a little" (Is. 28:10). This sounds reasonable and acceptable. God simply grows me up one step at a time. It should not be difficult.

There is a slight problem. The flesh, that spiritual and soulish part of us that has a tendency toward sin, cannot be grown into good. It cannot be reformed. "For if you live according to the flesh you will die; but if by the Spirit you put to death the deeds of the body, you will live" (Rom. 8:13). The flesh cannot be bridled. It cannot be educated. It cannot be grown into good. It must be "put to death."

And how do I put my flesh to death? "No man can look upon the face of God and live." There is only one solution for the lie, and that is truth, and truth brings death. The discipline discussed in Hebrews 12 and Proverbs 1 is but a tool in the hand of God to bring us face to face with truth.

Why do we need discipline? We need death to that portion of our flesh that has surfaced today. And death does not feel good. It does not feel like it comes from the God who loves us. Many are running around declaring all kinds of things to be of the devil. If these same persons would simply face some truth, they might see some real growth. Instead, the "attack of the enemy" is often but a diversion from "death to self."

Taking the Land

Conquering the flesh is not accomplished through a simple, single act of bravery. God illustrates what it is like to conquer the flesh through the entry of Israel into the promised land. Though He could have, God did not wipe out the wicked people for Israel and let Israel just waltz in to grab up a wide-open land. To do so would have left the land free for the wild animals and the weeds to take over. Moses tells the people, "And the LORD your God will drive out those nations before you little by little; you will be unable to destroy them at once, lest the beasts of the field become too numerous for you" (Deut. 7:22). Even the wicked people of the land exercised a certain amount of control over the land that was better than vacancy.

In the same way, God only challenges that part of our flesh where there is some potential of a good end result. If we are not poised and ready to "take the land," it does God absolutely no good to challenge a given area. If, however, our heart is ready to fill the void that would be created by the discipline of God with His life, then God is ready to act in a given area. He does not just indiscriminately wipe out areas of our flesh. It is dependent upon our willingness to be filled with His life.

Jesus illustrates this principle in Luke 11, describing what can happen when an evil spirit leaves a person:

> When an unclean spirit goes out of a man, he goes through dry places, seeking rest; and finding none, he says, 'I will return to my house from which I came.'
>
> And when he comes, he finds it swept and put in order. Then he goes and takes with him seven other spirits more wicked than himself, and they

> enter and dwell there; and the last state of that
> man is worse than the first. (v. 24-26)

The cleansing that God desires should be done with His help, and with an eye toward receiving more of His presence. Instead, people often try to "clean their own houses." They try to rid themselves of any wrongdoing and to then put on a good life. This will work for a season. At times it even lasts for years if the habits are strong enough and the society reinforces it. However, we are not designed to be filled with "good works" but with the presence of God Himself, which then produces the good works. The person who desires to be "good" in order to be seen, opens himself up to every kind of evil.

Many times this happens in churches. People fall in love with their own goodness, which is so much superior to what it was only a few years before. Forgetting that anything of value was accomplished in Christ, they begin "comparing themselves among themselves" (2 Cor. 10:12b). Because their house has been swept but is not being filled with His presence, pride enters. Division follows. Soon every evil thing begins to manifest (James 3:13-18).

God knows that the believer that grows too quickly can and will come under the influence of pride. The tendency to compare is simply too strong. In His wisdom, He takes us into our "promised land" one step at a time. He helps us occupy the land in such a way that we know we need His help to do it. He reminds us of our need to glorify Him each step of the way. He stands ready to do the work, but watches us to see if the humility is present that will cause the next step to be a blessing to all.

Even if God could somehow instantly cleanse every man, woman, and child, to do so would not be wise. The empty vessel is an open invitation to the demonic, just as much as it is to the holy. And the demonic will seize any part of the vessel that it can. God waits for an invitation. The devil dominates and manipulates. God cooperates with us in a perfect love relationship. The ground He takes is taken with mutual consent.

God cleanses a little at a time, and then waits for us to ask Him to fill the void. Today's portion of the flesh must die, so that today's portion of filling can take place. If there is no hunger to be filled by God, there really is no reason for God to even bother convicting us of an area of our flesh.

Often a believer will realize that there is a lack of conviction and that there is a kind of smug self-satisfaction in his walk. The mind of this believer tells him that something is wrong. Yet, lacking a true hunger for God, the solution is often self-conviction and self-cleansing, which simply leads to more pride and less of a hunger for God. How easily we can deceive ourselves!

If there is one condition that we should fear above all others, it is that we lack a hunger for God. There will always be a certain amount of flesh that we need to conquer. At a given point in time, God may or may not be convicting us of our sins. We may be in a season of discipline where we keenly feel the conviction, or we may be in a season of blessing where we are being encouraged. But one thing should be constant. We must desire more of Him!

If we are not careful, sin will romance us and take away our hunger for God. When the Spirit comes to challenge a given area, sin will maintain its hold and keep us "full." Sin will point us to our "good works" and to the wonderful way that we have grown. The Spirit points us to the goodness of God, and to our need for more of Him. Sin points us to self. The Spirit points us to God. The more we see of God, the more we want. The more we see of self, the less of God we want. Are you hungry to see God's face?

Strength Through Conquering

 Additionally, the people needed to conquer. Taking a land is essential to having value for the land that is taken. God does not hand us things on a silver platter. To do so would destroy us. He knows that we need to overcome. We need to actually fight for the very thing that He would willingly give us and could give us if He chose to. But He doesn't choose to because to choose to would keep us from developing the conquering strength in our hearts.

God led the nation of Israel into the promised land one battle at a time. As long as the nation of Israel stayed away from sin, covenants with the enemy, and the idols of the land, conquering was no problem. In short, the Israelites were practicing walking with God and conquering at the same time. Meanwhile, the evil nations that God desired to judge were being judged. The evil nations acted as "caretakers" until God's people were ready to assume control. Sometimes even a despot is better than total anarchy and confusion. Sometimes even some of the less destructive fleshly habits are better than what could replace them.

Just as the nation of Israel had to put to death the people of the land to inherit the land, so must we put to death the flesh to inherit our land. Whenever the people of Israel became friends with or made a deal with the people of the land, they got in trouble. The Gibeonites fooled them into making a covenant with them. Balak seduced the Israelites into sin through the women of his camp. Achan caused defeat through the taking of the Babylonian garments and of the gold and silver that were to be dedicated to God.

There is no reforming a perverted and grotesque flesh. We want to reform it. We think that God was evil for having the Israelites kill off the people of the land. But the people of the land had sunk to lows of sacrificing their own children to the gods, to grotesque idolatry, to witchcraft and to other spiritist ways, and to a perverted sexuality and lifestyle. The entrenched evil of the land could not be retrained. It had to be destroyed. So it is with our flesh. It cannot be retrained. It must be destroyed. Even the comparatively "good" flesh must eventually be destroyed to go deeper in God.

When God comes to destroy our flesh, He seems to be "no friend of mine." He seems unreasonable. He seems unloving. We see our good intentions and excuse our flesh as "slightly misguided." He sees a person headed for total rebellion and idolatry. "He who pampers his servant from childhood will have him as a son in the end" (Prov. 29:21). As long as we treat our flesh kindly, our flesh will end up inheriting all that we have. It will become "our son."

No man can see God in His glory and live. Praise the Lord! May we no longer see that as a threat but as a blessing. It is a scary thing to come before the glorified presence of our Lord and Savior. And it does bring death, but not eternal death. We are eternal beings that will never cease to exist. Eternal death is eternal separation from God. Gazing on Him does not bring eternal death but eternal life. It brings death to that part of us that keeps us from true life. Our flesh can and will die.

All of us will face God sooner or later. Those who have coddled the flesh will face much death at that time. Some will have no life left. They will be banished to the place of eternal death. Some will have much left. Why? Because they chose to face death now . . . death to self . . . and to grow an inheritance in the Son instead of in the self. No man can look upon God's face and live. Hallelujah! What a promise! Oh God! Let me see Your face!

Chapter Four

Fire

As I rounded the corner of our house, a million little torches spread from one end to the other of the old wooden barn. In seconds, the flames at the south end of the barn had completely engulfed the entire barn. I stood stunned. What could I do? "The tractor!" I heard my dad yell, but he was already off to get it moved back from the fire. I still stood motionless.

Then I saw the calves. They were trapped inside a fence just a few feet away from the incredible heat of the inferno. Instantly, I ran toward them empowered with an incredible adrenaline rush. I leaped the fence and started to grab for a calf to throw it over the fence to freedom. The calves, already crazy with fear, bolted back toward the fire. It was as if they didn't even know me.

I was finally able to catch one calf and then another. Even with the rain falling, the fire became unbearable. I leaped the fence to find a water puddle to roll in just to cool off. I was on the verge of serious burns from the heat, and still the calves would run back toward the fire. Finally, Dad came with some pliers and began cutting the wire.

Our only hope, as human beings, begins when we face the truth. Sin rages within us as a consuming fire that will destroy us. It is only a matter of time. The truth is our rescuer, and it comes wrapped in many different packages. Sometimes it is found in a book. Sometimes it comes through a friend. Other times, it is hidden in a major life happening. Yet, paralyzed with fear, we often run back into the fire.

One of the results of Adam's sin was a kind of insecure self-awareness. Adam realized that he was naked and was ashamed. What did he do? He hid. In a way, he tried to run back into the fire. He had sinned against God, and instead of returning to the only One who could help the situation, he ran farther into destruction.

The Guilt Factor

Self-esteem has become a buzzword in our society. The person with low self-esteem will never make the effort to do much of anything. Yet, in a fit of rage, this same person will lash out in a terribly destructive way trying to make up for the years of being trashed. The scene of an embittered employee firing off a gun randomly in a Post Office, a school, or a restaurant and then turning it upon himself is becoming all too common in our society. Feeling like a nobody is a disease that rages in our modern society, fueled especially by the break-up of the family unit.

The truth of God, at first, only seems to make it worse. If I start with low self-esteem, why would I want to have a revelation of the glory of God which only makes my sin that much more evident to me? Truth increases my pain to an even more intolerable level. It would seem that if I have any good sense at all, I would run from truth . . . right back into the fire.

And so it is that many run from the very truth that could set them free. Guilt does not feel good. Guilt on top of self-hatred and self-accusation is an intolerable combination that is simply too much for the human psyche to take. The self-preservation instincts will kick in and cause the person to run from the guilt, which seems to be the only force that the person can escape. Like the calves crazed with fear, the prospect of real freedom means nothing to the one already in pain overload. More pain simply cannot be tolerated. And if truth means pain, truth must go.

The teenage addict needs the truth of God's word, but all he can feel is the pain of not fitting in with the crowd. How does the truth of his needed changes sound to him? It sounds like a recipe for further isolation. What few "friends" he has will be lost if he gives up his habit. The truth appears to be an unbearable enemy.

The spurned woman is looking for love in all the wrong places. Loneliness grips her inner person with a deathlike hold. She hears that the truth declares her current relationship to be sin, but it really doesn't matter. There is no choice. Letting go of what little life she has is out of the question.

The bookkeeper's wife is sick and desperately in need of medicine. His personal finances have been drained. Nobody is looking over his shoulder at work. There is an easy solution. It seems right. It seems justified. He loves his wife. He must do what he has to do. Childhood training whispers to his conscience, but the voice is easily drowned out with the urgency of the moment. After all, wouldn't God want him to take care of his wife?

Impossible Challenge?

Knowing our tendency to run from the truth, God has a real challenge. How can He present the truth in such a way that those who need it the most can receive it? The very ones that need it the most are the most likely to run back into the fire. It would seem that only the marginally bound have a decent chance of facing truth and obtaining any real measure of the life that God has for them through His truth.

For starters, God cannot reveal ultimate truth to us. It must be dealt out to us in little increments that we can handle . . . "here a little, there a little" and "line upon line" (Is. 28:10). That is part of why He came as a man, a man who had totally laid aside His glory to become like one of us. He was giving us something we could handle.

Even more though, He came not just to confront and to convict but to enable. The truth is not nearly as threatening once you have begun to walk at least toward the right direction. The teenager gets a bad batch and ends up in the hospital. The needed change is staring him in the face. Through the hospital experience, he has already dried out once, so . . . . The woman, caught up in a wrong relationship, finds herself in the middle of a terrible fight. Things go sour. She has to start over anyway . . . and maybe . . . there is another way. The bookkeeper is facing strict new auditing procedures. Now it is not just extra income that is in jeopardy. A change is demanded . . . but what if they look back? Should I come forward or just hope . . .?

The ego can handle a rebuke once it is at least beginning to move toward the needed correction. In the same way, Jesus often leads us into partial obedience even before we begin to fully see Him in a given area. Among those who have come to

Christ, a testimony can frequently be given of His step by step leading even before salvation. Little by little, God leads us toward Himself at a time when we don't even recognize His drawing. Having already arrived near the destination, we "willingly" make the final decision.

It is much like the cutting down of the fence to get the calves away from the fire. He can perfectly remove the roadblocks, because He understands how we operate. He doesn't fight against our nature, but He works with it.

Just As If . . .

One of the most incredible statements of the Scriptures is "Abraham believed God, and it was accounted to him for righteousness" (Rom. 4:3b). A great longing of everyone of us is "to be able to get it right." We'd love to be "perfect" even if only for a day. Abraham wasn't perfect, but God "accounted to him" that perfection or "righteousness" that each one of us longs for.

I believe that one of the reasons we suffer so greatly from low self-esteem is very simply because we somehow do recognize internally just how far short of the mark we really fall. There is an image of what we should be inside us. There is also a longing to live up to that image.

One of Abraham's great longings was to be a father. He had no children, and in that day that was a great reproach. He fell short of the mark. It damaged his self-esteem. It was this deep longing within Abraham's heart that God appealed to as He began to call him out from among his people.

Did this one response make Abraham perfect? No way! Yet
the Scriptures tell us that as Abraham believed God and
responded to Him in this one thing, God "accounted it to him
for righteousness." God took the very thing that Abraham
wanted the most, used it as a lure, and then, when Abraham
responded, God called him "righteous."

How can God do this? Simple. Through the death of His own
Son, God has paid the penalty for sin. No sin we can do is
outside the payment zone. No billion dollar fine can be levied
that He is not rich enough to pay. All jail time has already been
served. And if death is needed, even that too has been taken
care of.

For Abraham, it meant a new and a fresh start. The slate was
wiped clean. Even though his family lived in a region that
worshiped false gods, and he may have even been involved in
the practice, God was able to say, "If you will follow me, I will
declare you righteous."

The sin part was and is completely taken care of. Even future
sins come under this incredible covering. No addict or murderer
has ever done anything outside of the payment zone of Christ.
His death makes it "just as if" they had never sinned.

Yet, the " if you will follow me" is very important, because it is
simply a new start. God is not interested in an empty slate. He
is not desiring a bunch of blank lives that are bearing no fruit.
In Luke 13, Jesus tells a parable of a tree that is not producing
any fruit. The tree could be compared to the wicked or anyone
else who is not producing any fruit for God. The command for
the tree is, "Cut it down."

We often think of ourselves as doing "many" good things. Yet
the Word of God declares that, "without Me, you can do

nothing" (John 15:5b). If we compare ourselves among ourselves, some of us look pretty good. Others look terrible. Yet, God's standard is different. His standard asks if we are declaring His lordship and His glory unto the earth and to the heavens. Everything of selfish or wicked motives will be washed away. Average human goodness no longer makes the grade. Apart from Christ directed responses, we cannot fulfill the first part of our purpose.

Thus God says of Abraham, "He responded to me. I will declare Him righteous." When we show forth God's glory and lordship through believing in Him and obeying Him, He wipes the slate clean and takes our one act as the beginning point of developing a truly fruit-bearing person. With our first response, He declares us "righteous." With our continuing responses, He truly "makes" us more and more righteous.

If someone starts out as a grotesque sinner, even after walking with Christ for a few years, he may not meet the "averages" of the righteousness of men very well. Even so, the slate is clean. Even so, God doesn't care about the averages. What He cares about is that His lordship and His glory is being revealed in and through that individual. The fresh start is moving toward real fruit and more and more of it.

Every day of his life, it is "just as if" he had never sinned. The death of Christ triumphs over sin. The "obedience response" establishes righteousness. It is an "obedience response" that establishes righteousness and not just a good work. An "obedience response" shows forth the glory of the Lord. A good work brings glory to the one who does it. A good work may do nothing but stroke a selfish ego.

God is no longer concerned about the average level of good in a person's life. The cross took care of that. He is very concerned about growth and fruit. He is concerned about truly cleansing the gross stuff out and putting more of His life and light in. And He knows that the one who is responding to Him will be transformed into His likeness. It is only a matter of time, and He has all eternity. The one who refuses to respond cannot and will not be transformed, not even in the space of eternity.

Is there anything more beautiful than the joyful smile of a young child? The child may not be able to walk, or feed himself, or have any control over his bowels. Yet, to us, he is perfect. New-born Christians are much like that. The glow of Christ is all over them. They are not yet walking in maturity. Areas of sin that God will one day challenge are somehow hidden in the background, while the glow of His presence is very real. They are not just "legally" perfect, but practically perfect through His presence.

Through the cross, Christ can legally declare us "clean" and "perfect" if we will only believe. Through His presence we can experience the gift of being a somebody, being His child. He offers total love and acceptance to those of low self-esteem, simply for the asking. Through faith, we receive a sense of His pleasure in us. The very thing that we desperately need, He gives us with no strings attached. Once again, where He could have easily condemned us, He works with our nature leading us with kindness, love, and acceptance.

Standing Between Us and the Fire

The barn fire was just too hot. I could not get between the calves and the fire. Thus they would run back into the fire. No human being has what it takes to rescue another man from sin. The fire is simply too hot. Only Jesus could take the heat. In the garden of Gethsemane and then on the cross, He took the heat. We can now run toward freedom instead of heading back into the fire.

With the love and acceptance we find in the cross, the self-esteem question is more than settled. Jesus loves us. He declares us to be His brothers and sisters, children of the Father. He makes it "just as if" we had never sinned on every day of our lives. He extends His help and His fellowship to us. Truth no longer needs to scare us. Jesus is the answer to any truth about our own sinfulness.

That is a great start! Yet, even then some of His beloved ones will still find the attraction to an embittered lover a stronger pull than the perfect love of an invisible God. The grip of past habits and of sin is great. More truth is needed.

Standing between His beloved "calves" and the fire, Jesus next uses our natural fears to cause us to run to freedom and away from sin. In some cases, that means that the hideousness of the habit must be exposed for what it is. The addict gets a "bad" batch. The lover becomes hateful. The attraction becomes repulsive.

That, in essence, is what Jesus does for us. He steps between us and our sin in a way that makes it easy for us to get to freedom. To stay in our sins, we must turn and run right over the top of Him. He uses our natural tendencies that once held us in sin, to cause us to move toward freedom.

For Abraham, God used the desire for children to draw Him out of bondage. Later, he used contention between Abraham and Lot to help Abraham fully obey the command to separate completely from his family. God turns the natural pulls that were once our enemies into our friends. They become the very forces that move us toward God instead of pulling us away from God.

He cuts down the fence. He destroys every bondage that could ever hold or limit us. Then He steps right in between us and the consuming fire of our sin. He became and still is our ultimate intercessor. He is both a shield and an encourager to us to leave the heat of the fire. And He sends the Holy Spirit to enable us to walk in truth. Jesus is the answer to truth.

Left to ourselves, none of us could escape. We need a rescuer. Truth, by itself, only destroys. It graphically illustrates how far we fall short of the glorious person that God created us to be. We need the enabling of the Holy Spirit.

Once we see truth, we need to know that God has the power to transform us into the image of truth. Truth alone brings condemnation. Truth with enablement brings transformation. Jesus tears down the fences and provides the way. Freedom is within our grasp!

Chapter Five

Receiving Truth

"The heart is deceitful above all things, and desperately wicked; who can know it? I, the Lord, search the heart, I test the mind, even to give every man according to his ways, according to the fruit of his doings" (Jeremiah 17:9-10).

None of us really wants to hear that the heart of man is "deceitful" and "desperately wicked." All over the world, philosophers and common men alike prefer to describe the innate goodness of man, as if it really were truth. We do not want to accept that what goodness we have would be turned to some selfish end if left to ourselves.

When Jesus was in Jerusalem, at a time when the people seemed to be in love with Him, the Scriptures say, "But Jesus did not commit Himself to them, because He knew all men, and had no need that anyone should testify of man, for He knew what was in man" (John 2:24-25).

Another year, Jesus would ride into Jerusalem amidst the "Hosanna's" of the crowd, only to be crucified in the same city just a few days later. If the crowd couldn't have a powerful leader to crush the Romans the way they wanted, the crowd would crush the potential leader. The selfishness of the crowd caused it to cry "Hosanna" to Jesus. The same selfishness caused the crowd to crucify Him. The illusion of the goodness of the crowd faded quickly.

Even the disciples, who were not a part of the cry of the crowd to "'Crucify Him!'" (Mark 15:13b), were touched by some of the same selfish motives. James and John get special notice for their selfishness when they ask for the priority position in Jesus' future kingdom (Mark 10:35-37). Yet, the other disciples are no better. James' and John's request caused the rest of the disciples to be "greatly displeased with James and John" (Mark 10:41). And why were they so displeased? Jesus did not grant the request. Their displeasure came because of their selfishness. Each of them wanted the best place in the kingdom. The log and speck principle came to life. Seeing a selfish request stirred the selfishness within each of them.

Even after the crucifixion, when the disciples should have been starting to understand that Jesus' kingdom is not of this world, the desire for a priority place in the kingdom still surfaces. Acts 1:6 records their response. "Therefore, when they had come together, they asked Him, saying, 'Lord, will You at this time restore the kingdom to Israel?'" This response can be taken as simple curiosity, but the fact that Jesus responds with "you shall receive power . . ." lets us know that the disciples are still looking for their payoff for the sacrifices they had made when they chose to follow Jesus.

Amazingly, Jesus accepts this selfishness as a part of the human condition. He doesn't even rebuke the disciples, but uses the desire for power to lure them toward His unseen kingdom. Jesus seems to acknowledge that instead of trying to completely purge the human heart, He must work with it to be successful in bringing redemption.

"The heart is deceitful above all things." That is Scriptural fact. For those who want to go deeper in God, this fact must be accepted, even embraced. We must understand that when truth comes to us, we won't understand. Our heart will take us for a ride. We will be sold down the river into the slavery of sin, and not even know that it has happened. So smooth is the deceit of the ego that the Scriptures say we are deceitful "above all things." It is our most predominant characteristic.

The Hypocrite on a Stage

How often have you watched a close friend or even an acquaintance that had a significant blemish in his or her personality, only to realize that the person didn't have a clue of the shortcoming? What's more startling, if the person does ever realize the shortcoming, he is totally shocked to find out that it is so obvious that everyone else already knew about it anyway. It is almost funny, at times, to watch people try to cover up some area of defect that virtually everyone who meets them can see with little more than a glance.

"The heart is deceitful above all things." So how do we overcome this tendency of the heart? The Psalmist answers that question: "Who can understand his errors? Cleanse me from secret faults. Keep back your servant also from presumptuous sins; let them not have dominion over me. Then I shall be blameless, and I shall be innocent of great transgression" (Psalms 19:12-13). The secret sins, or hidden sins, are those that are imbedded in our own hearts, but for whatever reason, we cannot see or have not acknowledged them yet.

Presumptuous sins are similar. We act on what we think to be
truth, only to find that our presumptions have been wrong.

"Who can understand his errors? Cleanse me from secret faults."
The Psalmist understands his own helplessness and his own
ability to deceive himself. He knows that only the truth of God
brought to him in the right time and the right way will make a
difference. He knows that he is helpless to battle what he cannot
even see unless God undertakes on his behalf.

From Presumption to Power Over Sin

This is the starting point of victory. James tells us that "God
resists the proud, but gives grace to the humble" (James 4:6b).
The one who thinks that he is a good man and able to perform
up to God's standard is proud. What better definition of proud
could you possibly give? The one who realizes that he is full of
sin and is utterly helpless to do anything about it is humble.
How can you get any more humble than admitting both
weakness and blindness to your own weakness?

As both the Psalmist and James point out, it is God who can and
will make the difference. God's grace brings both mercy and
enablement. Mercy is needed. Otherwise, we would simply
receive the wrath due us for living a lie. Enablement is needed.
Otherwise, we would simply continue to live just as we always
have, in greater and greater bondage to sin.

Yet it is not just God Who makes the difference. If that were so,
all of mankind would be redeemed. God's grace is for the
"humble." His cleansing is for those who admit their tendency
toward presumptuous and secret sins. He is most able and most

willing to help those who do not fight against Him when He comes.

When challenged, the ego is quick to do a survey of recent actions and words. It will then make a comparison with others and usually come up with a favorable pronouncement that it really is not doing that badly, comparatively. This natural tendency of the ego will kill the work of God. It is the opposite of humility and a rejection of total dependence on God to show us truth.

"The heart is deceitful above all things." Its first tendency is to defend itself. To grow deep in the Lord, that tendency must be disarmed. James says that "If anyone is a hearer of the word and not a doer, he is like a man observing his natural face in a mirror; for he observes himself, goes away, and immediately forgets what kind of man he was" (James 23-24). None of us measures up to the standards of the Word of God. Yet every one of us will, if left to self, forget that very fact and begin to defend our own goodness.

Complete Confession

Instead, we need to remember God's remedy, confession. A declaration of truth is both the goal and the answer. To live truth, we must first declare the truth of our present sinful condition: "If we confess our sins, He is faithful and just to forgive us our sins and to cleanse us of all unrighteousness" (1 John 1:9). We understand that this verse applies to salvation, but what about our daily lives? Another way to look at this verse would be to say that "To the degree that we confess . . .

we are cleansed." It is amazing that God gives us this kind of remedy. In a way, the results are in our own hands. If we choose to be fully open and honest, He can and will fully cleanse. If we hide or ignore things, we continue in much the same state that we started.

This does not mean that the blood of Christ is not sufficient to cover our sins. God's atoning work is able to cover all sins. A person can be saved and still not deal with every area of sin in his or her life. What it does mean is that the "tree" is not going to bear fruit the way it could have. In a given area, the sin is cutting off the flow of the Spirit. The branch is not plugged into the vine the way it could have been. Truth is not being fully declared by the believer because there has only been partial confession, partial honesty.

To think the only thing we can do is to confess and await His cleansing is very difficult for most to do. One of the hardest things we can ever do is to "stand still and see the salvation of the Lord." We want to be a part of our own salvation. We want part of the credit.

The ego, if given a chance, will confess . . . and then blame. It will take "its share" of the guilt. And it will get "its share" of the cleansing from the Lord. It is hard to stand and feel the accusing finger of the Lord without looking around and saying "But what about him?" It is even harder to feel the accusing finger of another person without turning a finger back at the accuser's sins which probably are very real and visible.

Yet, any deflection of the truth brings a deflection of the blessing. Any defense of self that turns the focus away from the truth about self ends up destroying the very purpose that God may have had in a given situation. He allows things to come into our lives to reveal hidden sins in our lives. If we respond with a humble and helpless confession, those sin areas are transformed into truth. If we deflect the blame, we remain almost just as we were.

The kind of growth God wants you to have will not come because of your own goodness or even from your own efforts. It will come when you cease striving to be good, disarm yourself, and receive the truth of God. We need to begin to let the events of life become our teacher. We must allow them to begin to reveal our hearts. The ego must be disarmed.

Though hard to take at times, a right response to the truth will be followed closely with a package of God's love, mercy, and His wonderful presence. Having received God's truth, and confessed it to be true, "then I shall be blameless, and I shall be innocent of great transgression."

Chapter Six

The Real Life Response

Truth is not the enemy. It just feels like it is. Honesty, really deep honesty, is the beginning point of every spiritual battle. When we want to defeat our spiritual enemy, Satan, all we need to do is to be honest. We simply speak the truth of God. Satan cannot prevail over truth. His power is in lies, secrecy, deception, intimidation and manipulation. Truth, spoken openly, destroys the power of the devil.

Truth spoken openly brings a humbling of the soul. Real truth puts us back into the perspective of being a servant of God. And while serving God is a high and lofty calling, the servant still must recognize his utter dependence on God. God is the creator of the universe. He is everywhere present at all times. One word from His mouth can shake the entire earth. One thought of His stands to all generations. Remove the sustaining power of God, and man collapses into dust, the earth becomes stillborn, and the sun, moon, and stars crash into a dead nothingness of space. What is man compared to God?

We need that perspective. We need that humility. We need honesty. We have been fed such a steady diet of "fairness" and of what we "deserve" that our egos are puffed up with a false self-importance. We think that we are something special because of what we do or who we are. In truth, we are something special, but it is because of Who created us and Whom we serve.

Honesty and humility are at the center of every spiritual victory. God promises to watch over the humble to lift them up (James 4:6). With humility, the battle is no longer our own; it is God's. With honesty, truth has a chance in our lives. God's life can begin to be manifested in and through us. How different that is from our own efforts to be good!

Beyond Theory

The battle begins. A word is spoken to me. I don't like it. I have been violated. I feel cheap and unappreciated. Is it truth or is it a lie? My own ego immediately judges it to be a lie and goes into action thinking of its own "truth statements" about the other individual. The fight is on, but the fight is wrong.

Truth is not just about facts. Truth is not about you vs. me. Truth is about manifesting the love and character of God. It is about living in a manner that will show to the world a picture of the incredible One who created us. The very battle that we think is about truth is actually distracting us from living the truth.

Satan's primary hope is to distract us, to get us to fight battles that we don't need to fight. If we ever really begin to fight in the manner that God has ordained, there is almost no fight to the battle. We speak and live the truth, and it dispels the darkness. If Satan can get us to compare ourselves with others, and to begin to shadow box with him and with other people, he knows that we will no longer be living the truth. He has won.

When a person speaks a word to us, Satan and his forces are right there trying to get us to relate to the situation as if we were the center, and not in a way that acknowledges that we are but one part of a manifestation of God's truth and glory. In simple words, he is stimulating our ego to go into action to defend self and to attack the other person involved. Once that battle is engaged, all Satan has to do is to sit back and watch. His work is all but completed.

A word is spoken to me. I don't like it. I acknowledge that I FEEL violated. I ask God why I feel that way. I ask God to speak truth to me and to reveal truth in me. I refuse judgments against the other person. I stand still and wait for the saving help of the Lord.

This may be the single hardest thing a person could ever do. It goes against all instincts. The ego vibrates rapidly and shakes, like a horse at the starting gate, wanting to be turned loose. It wants to be set free to do its work, but it must be chained. It must be quieted. It must be stopped in order to begin to manifest the peace and presence of God.

Most people expect the "answer" first. They want to know "Who's right" and "who's wrong." "Where am I right?" and "Where is the other person wrong?" The first answer that comes is the peace of God in our spirits. The first answer that comes is a manifestation of truth into our lives. And if we let that peace do a complete work in us, often it no longer matters "Who's right?"

Usually, though, once the peace gets there, we are deceived to believe that we have conquered totally, and then we let the ego go back to work analyzing and "setting the record straight." In a matter of moments, we have returned to an egocentric person who is no longer manifesting the truth of God. Yet, we feel so justified because we were restrained in our actions and because we compare so favorably to the one that insulted us. Our ego admires its own spiritual accomplishments in the face of adversity. Truth began. Deception entered. Truth lost.

The Ego vs. the Truth

Truth is first and foremost a manifestation of the character of God. The ego has no part in truth. It puts us at the center and denies that God is the all-sustaining One. Honesty brings the work of the ego to a screeching halt. It refuses to take up the battle of self-defense. It teams up with humility to receive the peace of God. It then asks God for a search of self for hidden sins, knowing that self-deception is our most prominent characteristic. And it waits. No other response is needed. No other response is wanted– until God speaks.

Matthew 7 tells us to first take the log out of our own eye and then take the speck out of the other person's eye. Humility and honesty does not mean that we will never give an answer back to the one that has insulted us. It does mean that it will be done with the delicate sensitivity that we would use to take a speck of dirt out of the eye of another person. Why? Because we are dealing with a person's ego. And hopefully our goal is to have truth manifested in both of us, not just in "me" so that "I" will have bragging rights. A delicate reply is much less likely to set the defenses in motion that will inevitably bring out the lie in the other person. We must want truth to be manifested.

The True Battle

The battle is whether or not we will manifest the truth of God. Honesty keeps the battle focused in the right direction. Humility allows God to intervene. God brings the victory. He gets all the glory. We rejoice in Him. We have nothing in the whole process that will feed our own egos. Self is brought to a standstill. God is exalted.

The active ego cannot stand this process. It chooses a path of religion. It gets busy in some good path for which it can take credit. It busies itself unto self-justification, that it might compare favorably with the one who has injured it. It becomes the center of the universe. In its seeming goodness, it lives a lie.

Honesty is the battle. Can you stop the illusory battles long enough to receive what you need to fight the real battle? God's truth awaits the still vessel.

Chapter Seven

Embracing God

So far, this book has been laying some foundations of understanding, and it has been heavy on head knowledge. To go deeper in the Lord does not require more head knowledge but more of the power and authority to live a godly life. The authority to live out truth does not come from head knowledge but from an intimate interaction with God that is embraced by an individual and then is incorporated into an ongoing lifestyle.

Which comes first, the chicken or the egg? Which comes first, the thoughts in the head or the knowledge in the heart? We have been taught that we read it in a book and then we use that to change what is in our hearts. I believe that is often backward. What is going on in our inner spiritual parts, in our hearts, actually has the greater impact on what goes on in our heads and not the other way around.

The person with bitterness in his heart needs only the slightest provocation to set off a major onslaught of hateful thoughts.

The person feeling love and compassion would endure the same slight, hardly even noticing what had happened, and certainly without giving it any ongoing attention. The difference between the two is what is in the heart. The mind of the bitter person thinks that it is seeing the situation accurately, with great wisdom and self-control.

Though we don't realize what is happening, much of the thinking of the head is little more than a defense of the lifestyle that the heart is living. With the help of our deceitful and self-centered ego, our heart produces thoughts which primarily justify wherever the heart is at a given time.

It is not uncommon to find people who have grown up in the church, suddenly denouncing the strict moral code of their youth. Interestingly enough, their behavior has also gone through a change. People who would never have thought of living together without being married suddenly can find all kinds of reasons why this is acceptable, once the behavior is under serious consideration. The heart chooses a behavior. The mind rationalizes it. The body surrenders to it. Body, soul, and spirit are in unity. The person is deceived into thinking all is at peace.

The Other Way to Change Your Thought Life

It is possible, but difficult, to change your thinking and keep it changed long enough to impact what is going on in your heart. It is a much simpler route to receive a heart change directly from God, which will almost instantaneously and effortlessly produce a new way of thinking. If you don't believe me, talk to someone who has been through a genuine conversion that deeply touched his heart.   Ask him if his thought life didn't go through an immediate and unexplainable change!

If you really want to go deeper with God, you may need to put down this book from time to time and truly experience from God the concepts that are being discussed.   One touch from God will bring a greater understanding of the things of God than several hours of deep thinking could ever bring.   If you let God change your heart first, your mind will come along quickly.   If you demand complete and total understanding, you will struggle.

Because we are so egocentric, we understand best what we have already experienced.   It would be nice if it were not so.   God knows that it is so.   Instead of condemning us for it, He draws us into Himself, and having experienced more of Him, our egocentric nature begins to work for us, producing an intellectual understanding of where it is and where it has been.

Recognizing the Real Enemy

The catch here, is that when God begins to draw us into Himself, we often react as if He were the enemy.   Isaiah 59:1-2 says, "Behold, the LORD'S hand is not shortened, that it cannot save; Nor His ear heavy, that it cannot hear.   But your iniquities have separated you from your God; And your sins have hidden His face from you, so that He will not hear."

Holiness absolutely scares unrighteousness.   For unrighteousness to exist, there must be a wall of protection.   Remember that the ego is busy thinking thoughts that justify where it is.   Those thoughts form a wall of protection that is very hard to penetrate.

If God were to try to draw near, the wall would begin to be destroyed. The ego reacts to God as an invading enemy.

Anytime God comes near, the mind and the emotions will have a strong urge to sound the alarm, to set off loud sirens, and to create a clamor of confusion that will distract the heart away from the invading force. As a person approaches salvation, there is often an incredible war going on. The easiest thing to do would be to run. And many do run many times before any significant breakthrough ever occurs.

The change comes when the Holy Spirit is allowed residence long enough to allow His presence to begin to impact the person's heart. The person senses how different his heart is from the heart of God. He senses that he falls short of the image of the glory that God has created for him. He wants what God has for him. The experience brings the desire.

Allowing God to Find Us

We have it backward. We think that we come to God. John 6:44 tells us that no man can come to Jesus unless the Father draws him. God comes to us. If we give Him enough space to co-exist with us, for even a time, it will begin to change us. We will then begin to respond, in our egocentric way, thinking that we are coming to God, not realizing that we have been changed by Him and are now able to take some feeble steps toward Him.

Too often, we do not allow God to get even that close. "No man can look at God and live." Our person cannot experience God and have the self stay intact as it was. The arm of God is not shortened, but our sins keep Him at a distance. We want to keep our self just as it is. In short, we love ourselves.

God's only hope is to rock our comfortable little worlds, to challenge our love of self. That is not hard. One selfish person can and will easily rock the world of another selfish person. God doesn't even have to actively intervene. The sins of man begin to batter and bruise one another until even the self-justifying ego cannot stand the way things are. The pain is intolerable. And the self-love of the ego causes it to begin to seek a more comfortable place to rest.

It is at this kind of time, that most will at least haltingly welcome the presence of God. Even though it is foreign and scary and different, it at least offers some hope of comfort. And yes, there is the prospect of the self seeing some of its own ugly selfishness by comparison with the loving presence of God. But even that is okay if it will just bring a relief from some of the pain. Our desire to get rid of the pain teams up with our love of self to temporarily embrace God.

Making God More Than Just a Pain Reliever

Unfortunately, this is the only time that some will allow God to come near. He is never actively and ongoingly embraced. Snatches of pain relief are all that are allowed. Maturity never comes.

Israel gives us a picture of this throughout the book of Judges. The people would chase after sin. God would give them over to an oppressor. The people would cry out to God. God would deliver them. The people would chase after sin, and the cycle would be repeated. God's truth and life was seldom seen in the people. The deeper walk was nowhere to be found.

Perhaps this is also a picture of you. Is your relationship with God one of crying out to a deliverer? Relief will come. Maturity will flee. And you will continue to live out primarily the lie before your fellow man, before the angels, and before God. You will fall far short of what God has created you to be: a reflection of His glorious character.

What is needed is an ongoing embrace of the presence of God. What we desire is some work that we can do and have it over with. We want to pray the right prayer or do the right act of obedience and declare ourselves whole. After all, if there is something that we can do to get right with God, even that strokes our ego and gives us a sense of being in control of our own destiny.

The idea of needing to helplessly wait in the presence of God just isn't appealing. The idea that it is God that must draw us or we don't have a chance is hard for the self-loving person to take. But it is Scripture and it is truth.

Are you reading this book hoping to find some knowledge key that will put you in the driver's seat, that will give you the power and authority you have been missing, so that you can take control and live a godly life? You will be greatly disappointed. There is no such key. The knowledge that the Scriptures speak of is a personal knowledge, like that of knowing a person. It is not knowing about God. It is not knowing information. It is knowing God.

To be more accurate, it is allowing God to come and abide for a period of time and to give Him the kind of attention that He deserves. It is more His effort to know us that brings our knowledge than our effort to know Him. It is far more His coming, with us merely receiving and embracing, than it is our doing. We really are mostly helpless. But, praise God, He is ready and waiting to come to us. Our openness will be rewarded.

The Experience of Abiding

If you begin to call upon God to come to you, several predictable things can and will happen. The first mistake is to be too active. We really are helpless. He must come to us. He must meet us where we are. We do not have what it takes to go to Him.

Often, people pour out great energy praising or thanking God or repenting, thinking that it will make a great difference. Each of those things is legitimate at the right time. But self-effort will not bring the presence of God. The presence of God is much more likely to be felt with a quieting of the soul than with an activating of every energy to try to bring on the presence of God.

Real praise, thanksgiving, and repentance will come as a **result** of God's presence. Human induced praise, thanksgiving, and repentance is just that. It is human induced. It is a function of self. And the soul will take credit for its great achievement in seeking God. And God will look on from a distance, knowing that the soul that glorifies itself, even for doing all the right things, cannot show forth the truth that God is the center and the sustainer of all things. The soul, while praising God outwardly, is inwardly taking credit for its good works and is not really a picture of the true praise of God.

This is the danger of human induced praise. Certainly, some praise can turn us toward the presence of God. It can prepare our hearts to embrace Him and as such is very helpful in opening up a flow of the Spirit of God. However, when praise becomes a magical work that gives us the control of forcing God's presence to show up, it has become perverted. The same is true of thanksgiving or repentance.

Thus, one of the greatest needs is to still the soul. Gentle, non-aggressive praise, thanksgiving, and repentance can be helpful, as long as it is moving the person toward receiving of God's presence, and it doesn't replace the need for God. Human induced praise can change the mood of the person which then causes him to think that everything is fine. In reality, there has been no spiritual change because there has been no presence. Only the emotions were affected.

The presence of God can begin as a gentle embrace, but often the first thing that you will feel is a very uncomfortable, dry, and almost confusing feeling. This should not surprise us. Anytime that we are in any degree of an unclean state before God, we are somewhat incompatible with Him. Some of our walls will have to be torn down. Some of our wonderful buildings will have to be destroyed. They are temples erected to self. We sense what God is about to do, and it is uncomfortable.

Many lose it at this point. For them, God is a feel-good God. Discomfort is displaced with praise or some other activity and the Spirit is quenched. God's Spirit brings death to self, and if we reject that death, we reject God. No religious activity will bring Him back.

A serious dedication to religious activity will give a person the illusion of real change. In reality, he is building shrines of self-effort to his own goodness. Many who reject God's Spirit will become great shrine builders, and to the casual observer they look good. But where are humility, long suffering, love, and a depiction of our utter dependence on God?

God brings death to self. Anything less is religious effort and will lack true spiritual authority. There is no other pathway to a real flow of God's presence. When we allow Him to bring death to self, we will live to God. We must embrace the discomfort God brings.

Certainly, after we allow God to do His work, the comfort sets in. But it only comes to those who mourn. It only comes to those who experience death. There is a human comfort from human words and human effort, and there is a God comfort that follows a death to self. To stay on the pathway to maturity in Christ, the believer must learn the difference.

By now, we can begin to see how easy it is to reject God and to embrace self-effort. Add in the deceitfulness of the heart and it is a wonder anyone ever grows at all. But Jesus has said that He will build His church, and build it He will. Our efforts are feeble, but God is mighty.

Philippians 1:6b tells us that "He who has begun a good work in you will complete it until the day of Jesus Christ." In Philippians 2:13, Paul continues saying, "for it is God who works in you both to will and to do for His good pleasure." Certainly these verses do not remove our responsibility to cooperate with God, and we can frustrate the work that He is desiring to do in us. But it is refreshing to know that the God of the universe is at work, overcoming some of the foolish things in our lives that would hinder us from growing in Him.

If our growth were up to us, we would be in trouble. But it is not. We are God's workmanship, if only we will cease striving and let Him work. The fruit of His workmanship will produce a good crop: thirty, sixty, and one hundred fold. Get ready for real growth!

Chapter Eight

Seeds of Truth

So you ask yourself, "How do I really know? My own heart will lead me astray at times. Even when I know the truth, I will be inclined to avoid it if it is an area that will cause me pain. How can I really know if I am seeing and responding to truth?"

Matthew 12:34b-35 give us an answer: "For out of the abundance of the heart the mouth speaks. A good man out of the good treasure of his heart brings forth good things, and an evil man out of the evil treasure brings forth evil things." The heart is invisible. The things we do and say are not invisible. The things of the heart will be made visible by what we do and say.

Our words and our actions become almost like a stage that brings to life for us and for the whole world those things that are within us. Often, we are the ones who are the most surprised at the scene that goes on. The world looks on with an unbiased viewpoint, unlike our own egos, and often could say, if we would only listen, "That is consistent with who you are."

A Picture from Nature

The things we do and say come from the "abundance" or the "overflow" of the heart. Nature illustrates this principle well. There are many seeds present in the soil at any given time. Most of those seeds remain invisible to the casual observer. In fact, if we were to begin to take some soil and sift it carefully, we still could not find all the seeds that are hidden even in a little section of ground.

Yet, when the weather conditions are right, and one of these little seeds begins to grow, it is obvious to even a little child that something is now there. And it came from a seed that up until that time had been completely invisible.

Scientists tell us that there are seeds in the desert that can lie dormant for hundreds of years. Then, when the needed moisture comes, the seed will quickly spring to life producing more seeds which in turn may wait another hundred years to grow and produce more seeds. During the time of "abundance," the seeds grow. During the time of drought, the seeds remain hidden.

So it is with our hearts. What we say and do are the result of a combination of a seed with a time of abundance. Our hearts are eternal beings created by God with an infinite capacity to store the spiritual seeds that are planted in its soil.

Those seeds come from everywhere. Some are planted directly by God Himself at the time of our creation and throughout our lives as He intervenes and comes to be with us and to teach us. Many are planted by other people and situations that we encounter just by living. Still others are sown into us through the spiritual heritage that comes from our parents and families. Even the spiritual realm around us has an impact upon our hearts, sowing seeds into our hearts. The number of seeds within our hearts are more than the sand of the seashore. The seeds that grow are those that are in their time of "abundance."

Again, nature can teach us much about our own hearts. Soil that is left bare will not stay bare for long. In the spring, one type of weed will begin to grow. When the weather turns hot, that weed will usually begin to die off, only to be replaced by another weed that grows well in the hotter weather. Toward the fall, yet another type of weed may emerge and become dominant in that same patch of soil. Only a fool would rejoice and declare the early spring weed gone because the summer has come. It will return next spring when the conditions of "abundance" for that particular weed have returned. Until then, it remains hidden.

What surfaces in our lives is a combination of a seed with a time of abundance. What is "growing" at a given time is not the sum total of our hearts. It is only what is presently abundant. Our goal should be to grow a fertile, lush lawn that is completely covered with grass or God's good for our lives. When one particular plant is in abundance, it tends to crowd out all other plants that would attempt to grow in that area. It does not mean that the weeds are not present. They just lay dormant and hidden. A thick and fertile lawn does not have weed problems, not because there is no weed seed, but because the lawn's abundance means that it is not the time of abundance for anything else.

So it should be true of our lives as they are constantly consumed with the things of God. Just as grass is one of the few plants that will crowd out the weeds, so too is a steady diet of the things of God the only real cure for the sin that would overtake us. Many have tried sports, or educational activities, or numerous other things to keep their children "out of trouble." Certainly, those things do take up space on our "lawn" and do have some value in preventing all-out weed growth. However, only the things of God will truly cover the space in a way that will stop the growth of the weeds.

Seeds of the Society

If we stop to think of the influences around us, each of us is a product of our society. Through experiences, seeds have been planted within each one of us whether those seeds are manifesting or not. Thank God, in many cases, the time of abundance has never materialized in our lives. By His grace, we have never let the weeds go to seed in a given area and as such have never really been significantly impacted by some of the sins of our generation. But he who thinks he is free of that influence is a fool.

In Adam's sin, we all sinned. To many, that is just an idle Scripture, but it is a description of spiritual truth. Have you ever said to yourself, "I wonder where that came from?" in response to something that was seemingly out of character? The truth is that it came from a seed that had been planted in your spiritual soil. And for whatever reason, a sufficient time of abundance finally occurred and the seed grew.

Perhaps now you can begin to see just how vulnerable you really are and just how much you need God. The fertile lawn is your only real hope. And the fertile lawn is God's seed of truth growing on the landscape of your life: watered, fertilized and weeded by Him. How much we need His seed to grow in us and to produce a good harvest!

Chapter Nine

Becoming a Person of Substance

As Westerners, we have been well schooled in the practical things of life. What we can feel, hear, touch, measure, and repeat in an experiment has been declared to be the stuff of truth. The concept of spiritual seeds planted in the invisible soil of the heart is not especially compatible with a Western way of thinking. Even as believers, we have tried to turn salvation and the things of God into four easy steps of action or a set of spiritual disciplines to be followed. Our minds simply relate better to the tangible and measurable because of how we have been taught to think.

Hebrews 11:1 says, "Now faith is the substance of things hoped for, the evidence of things not seen." In a Western way of thinking, that is about as much of a nonsense statement as a line from Lewis Carroll's "Jabberwocky": "Twas brillig, and the slithy tothes / Did gyre and gimble in the wabe."

"Faith," which is invisible, is the "substance" or the thing of real weight and tangible stuff, at least as compared to hope which is of less "substance" than that of faith. To the Western mind, which is used to having concrete things to work with, it is very confusing.

To begin to understand the Scriptures, we must first understand that the invisible realm is actually more real than the visible realm. As a Christian, which do you believe will last forever: your body which is visible, or your soul which is invisible? Which of the two is more real? The next verse after the "faith" verse says "the things which are seen were not made of things which are visible" (Heb.11:2b). God, Whom we cannot see, through His Spirit, Whom we cannot see, made everything that we can see. So which is more real: the seen or the unseen?

As Christians, there is no doubt about the answer. As Westerners, there is much discomfort about some of its implications. Suddenly, the things that matter the most are things that we cannot even adequately describe, nor can we give a set of steps to get us to an understanding. It is an invisible something that has "substance," and when you have it, you know it . . . at least hopefully you know it!

Do you have Jesus in your heart? To the typical Western mindset, that is nonsense. How can a person who lived and died dwell in another person? It contradicts the scientific principle that no two things can occupy the same space at the same time. To a Christian, that is barely a first base understanding.

Faith is the "Yes" our invisible part says to the moving of God upon us. Something within us "hears" or "sees" or "feels" the moving of God in such a way that our invisible part really is changed and the result is faith.

In Abraham, that faith caused him to leave the land in which he was living and head in the general direction that God had pointed him, not knowing anything about where he would end up. That same faith allowed him to take his son Isaac up on a mountain and to prepare to kill him just as one would an animal sacrifice. Why would he do such an insane thing? Because of some invisible "voice" that he had heard. Why did he not kill Isaac? Again, the "voice" spoke and stopped him.

Abraham's story, told in this way, sounds almost like a farce to the Western mind. Yet, we have no difficulty understanding the incredible power of the "character" of a man. As a young athlete, I remember the phrase posted on the wall, "When the going gets tough, the tough get going." What do you have on the inside? In a time of testing, it will clearly manifest itself! The entrepreneur may be beaten down several times, but in the end he triumphs. The true champion fails over and over again, but when the title is on the line, he comes through. It is a question of that invisible stuff within.

Receiving the "Faith Substance" from God

In the same way, faith is a part of your substance within. But faith is different. It is not just a part of your invisible person, as much as it is the response of your invisible person to the working of God within you. Hebrews 11 says that because of God's working to bring faith in peoples' lives, they

> subdued kingdoms, worked righteousness, obtained promises, stopped the mouths of lions, quenched the violence of fire, escaped the edge of the sword, out of weakness were made strong, became valiant in battle, turned to flight the armies of the aliens. Women received their dead

raised to life again, others were tortured, not accepting deliverance, that they might obtain a better resurrection. Still others had trial of mocking and scourgings, yes, and of chains and imprisonment (v. 33b-36).

And the story goes on!

These men and women did not necessarily start with what they needed to complete the great works that they did. But through "faith", through saying "yes" to the invisible moving of God within them, they received what they needed to do feats above and beyond what a person could normally do. Some of those feats could simply be classified as extraordinary human accomplishments. Others required the supernatural moving of God to complete.

Abraham was willing to sacrifice his son because he had the promise from God that Isaac would be his heir and he believed God. Though it did not make sense to him, if God wanted him to kill Isaac, he must do it. Abraham went ahead with what he believed God had told him, thinking that evidently God must want to raise Isaac from the dead (Hebrews 11:19). In the end, the whole story becomes a perfect picture of what God would do for us in sacrificing His son, Jesus, on the very mountain where Abraham was being asked to sacrifice his son. Abraham passed a test of faith, and foreshadowed the goodness of God to us.

Abraham could not have gone ahead without believing that the same supernatural God that had spoken to him could and would intervene supernaturally again. Faith is not just a present day "yes" response to God, but it also carries with it a sense that God will return to do for me what I need now and in the future.

Daniel went calmly into the lion's den and stopped the mouth of the lions. The Shunamite woman refused to accept the death of her young son that God had supernaturally given her and pressed on until Elisha came and restored life to her son. Elijah spoke of rain to come and continued in prayer until the sign of a cloud was given. The rain came.

From Receiver to Participant

Faith is not just a response to God, but an activator of the power of God. A response to God brings a response from God, which sets in motion a continuous cycle that theoretically should never stop . . . unless or until we stop responding. The day we say "No" to God, we are once again limited to the invisible stuff that is inside us. At any given point, some of our inside stuff is good. Some of it is bad. The circumstances of our lives will create a "time of abundance" that will cause different things to manifest.

Without God, we are mostly helpless to do anything about some of the things we do and say. Our one hope is to manipulate the circumstances to keep as much good flowing as possible. In many cases, people are satisfied with the result and declare that they do not need God.

If there really is a heaven and hell, it is the mercy of God to bring a person to the "end of himself," so that he recognizes just how desperately he needs God. How much better it is to find that out now than on the day of judgment!

Going deeper in the things of God does require real change. It requires the kind of faith that opens up to God and says, "Yes, I am willing." It requires the kind of faith that says, "I am not satisfied with the good that you have created in me. I need God to help me become the person that I want to be." It is not willing to be limited to self. It cries out for more of God. At times it does require sacrifices that are not logically based, unless the invisible realm were to suddenly become visible and real. If we could only see the hearts as God sees them, everything would make so much more sense.

Faith comes from hearing. Hearing requires listening. Do you really want to go deeper? Put off the busyness of this life and begin to spend time waiting and listening. The flesh will scream with cries of needed self-efforts toward being good, but just still your soul and wait. Wait until you can't stand it any more and are ready to declare it a foolish waste of time. Then wait some more. When the flesh finally quiets down, the still, small voice of God will be waiting for you. It is that still, small voice that will make you a person of real substance, of real faith!

Chapter Ten

On Meditation

For most Westerners, the art of waiting and listening is an exercise in futility and frustration. Our invisible stuff has been well-programmed with the need to be busy and productive. If our busyness truly was productive, that would be great, but on God's scale of what is most real and most important, it is not true. Many of our most important works will simply burn on judgment day. We will get to see major segments of our lives evaporate into the nothingness that they really are in God's sight.

Because of its association with Eastern religions, meditation is in disrepute in many Christian circles. Using the same logic, prayer should be banned in the Christian religion, but it certainly has not been thrown out. Most Eastern forms of meditation begin with an emptying of self. At this point, Eastern and Christian meditation do have something in common. Christ said very clearly and several times that in order to find Him you would have to die to your own self.

Even at a very human level, the person that is "full of himself" only uses others as a sounding board for his own thoughts and boasts. In the end, that person usually has the illusion of having built relationships with others, when at best, he has a handful of acquaintances that have been tolerant of one-sided tirades. A real relationship means that there is a real exchange on the part of both parties involved.

Being full of sin and self, that is how we tend to come to God. In that mode, prayer is a rather one-sided affair, with us pouring out our hearts to God. And we do feel better. We are like a tea kettle that has blown off its steam, and with that completed, the conversation is over.

Meditation is different. Meditation is concentration on something other than self. In Psalms 1, the psalmist says, "Blessed is the man who walks not in the counsel of the ungodly, nor stands in the path of sinners, nor sits in the seat of the scornful; but his delight is in the law of the Lord, and in His law he meditates day and night" (Ps. 1:1-2). The man "delights" in the law of the Lord. He "meditates day and night." He concentrates on it. He digests it. It is his entire focus.

Eastern meditation is different. The goal, in at least some forms, is to get to a point of passivity or nothingness. The result is an openness to the spirit world which can be taken advantage of by any of the dark spiritual world.

For the Christian, quieting all the pushes and pulls and getting to a point of openness to the spiritual realm is not a bad thing. The Christians have a seal and a protection that the non-Christians do not have, especially as the believers turn their focus to Christ and to His law. The spiritual openness actually enhances the believer's ability to hear.

Fasting is similar. The believer makes an arbitrary choice not to listen to the desires of the body but to focus on the things of God. Certainly, at times, fasting is nothing more than a religious work done out of duty, but done correctly, fasting brings a spiritual openness that allows God a much freer interaction in our lives.

Again, the cults and the demonic realm have also made much use of fasting because it works to open up the spiritual realm. That does not make fasting evil nor is an openness to the spiritual realm evil. What is evil is opening up to something other than the Spirit of God.

Sidetracked by Seeing

Openness to the spiritual realm is just what it says it is. The believer is often more aware of Satan and his imps as well as of God and His angels. He also becomes much more aware of the "stuff" that is within him. In fact, times of meditation or times of fasting can bring some of the most disgusting "stuff" to the surface in the believer.

Here is where it is easy to get sidetracked. We are often so shocked by what we see surfacing from within us that we turn our attention away from God to try to hide or to get rid of the "stuff" we see surfacing. Satan works in a similar way. Since we can sense his presence more keenly than we normally can, he too tries to divert our attention away from God. He has little or no power over us at that point, but he is able to distract us from our goal: meditation upon God.

Seeing is Becoming

What we meditate on, we become like. It is an incredible instrument of change. First John 3:2b says "for we shall be like Him, for we shall see Him as He is." Somehow, what we "see" translates into a change in us. Most of us meditate on the things of this world by default. We do not actively choose what we are going to meditate on, and by default our system ends up meditating on wounds, problems, or earthly dreams. And the power of meditation transforms us into the image, not of Christ, but more into a man of this world.

If it is truly our desire "to be like Him," we have a great need to "see Him" on a regular basis. What we "see" day in and day out is going to determine what we will be. Opening up the spiritual channels to God is absolutely vital to going deeper in Christ. We must be changed. We must be transformed in the inner man. Through focusing intently on the Word of God, the person of Christ, and the works of God, we can become more like Him.

For most of us, trained in being useful or at least in being busy, meditation is a time to crawl the walls. To sit still and to stay focused on God is one of the hardest things a "productive" person can do. Spiritually, it is one of the most effective agents of change. To do nothing but to sit and meditate on the things of God gives a value to God that simply cannot be achieved by thinking on God . . . **and** something else. As "productive" people, we are willing to meditate while driving, or while shopping, or while . . . . But God is asking, how much do you value me? Am I worthy of your undivided attention?

Meditation, like prayer, is most effective when done as a discipline. It is good to have a regular time and place to spend with God at the center of your focus. A time of emptying of self will likely be necessary, but that is not meditation. It is preparation for the true meditation, which has God totally at its center. While I am about the business of confessing my sins, I have as a part of my focus, myself. I must get beyond that point. The goal in meditation is to put God at the conscious center.

The Role of the Word in Meditation

At times, the Word of God can be a real catalyst in meditation. But using the Word of God as an intellectual study is not the goal of meditation. Seeing God is the more accurate goal. An activity that is long on intellectual effort and short on seeing God and experiencing His presence really is not meditation but a religious exercising of the mind. Human effort in meditation will produce the fruit of spiritual pride and a tendency toward divisiveness and intolerance. True meditation will result in a greater humility and sense of needing the rest of the body of Christ. God's influence brings interdependence not isolation.

The Word of God should be, to us, a key to the door of the heart of the One we love. Just as we would read a love letter to find out what was in the heart of our lover, so should we meditate on and pour over the words of our Lord. Our primary goal should be to know Christ. We need to see Him. It needs to become so real that we can almost put out our hand and touch and taste what is happening in the Scriptures. Is that not what it is like when we read a letter of one we love? Do we not see the person saying different phrases? Do we not picture even the facial expressions and every little detail as if we were right there with him?

This is true meditation. It opens the door to God. And it is not just an exercise of self. It is guided by the Holy Spirit as we invite His presence to come and to guide us:

> But the anointing which you have received from Him abides in you, and you do not need that anyone teach you; but as the same anointing teaches you concerning all things, and is true, and is not a lie, and just as it has taught you, you will abide in Him (1 John 2:27).

This Scripture very much combines the "abiding" in Christ with the "anointing" in us. The Scriptures are understood through the influence of the Spirit upon us, an influence that happens over a period of time as we "abide" in Him. To me, that is an excellent definition of meditation. To abide means to dwell, to linger in one place even to the point of making it a permanent residence. Meditation is a lingering in the presence of Christ, and under the guidance of His Spirit, even to the point of making it a permanent residence.

From Discipline to Daily Presence

Meditation begins as a discipline of focusing on God during certain times but ends as a dwelling place at all times. It begins in isolation and total focus, and that sacrifice is needed. But it is not fully contained in the times of isolation. Indeed, the psalmist in Psalms 1 meditates "day and night." It becomes an unceasing interaction with God. It is our "focus time" with the One we love most. It brings to an end our love affair with self.

Instead of thinking continually and only self-centered thoughts, we begin to think God-centered thoughts. Instead of feeling and experiencing our own point of view, we begin to see and feel God's point of view. We do begin to love God "with our whole heart, soul, and mind." We even begin to "love our neighbor as ourself." After all, which of us can honestly say that we think and feel the thoughts of our neighbor or of God more than we think and feel the thoughts of self? Oh God, may I learn to meditate on you!

Chapter Eleven

The Right Stuff

"So why can't I just change?" you might be thinking. Certainly we see people all around us all the time making changes for the better, and they do so seemingly without the help of God. While such changes are difficult, they can happen. It is basically a question of "seed" and a "time of abundance." What is in the heart will eventually show up in the behavior of the person when the conditions are right.

Many entrepreneurs have the inner-drive it takes to succeed. They have the spiritual "stuff" or the "seeds" for success, but they fail over and over again until the right conditions arrive and incredible breakthroughs to riches arrive. In the same way, President Abraham Lincoln had the stuff of greatness within, but lost election after election en route to his successful bid for the Presidency. While President, his true greatness was evident for all to see.

Too often, we deal with surface issues, like smoking, or drinking, or even an inability to keep a house clean, when we need to focus more on the "real" issues of the spiritual realm. The "stuff" within your spirit will surface in a time of abundance, whether it is good or bad. The "stuff" in our spirit is probably THE single most important influence that needs to be dealt with in our lives if real change is to take place.

Once again, I come back to Abraham. Throughout the book of Genesis, God is very clear with Abraham that he is to leave the land of his fathers, to leave his family, and to never go back. That may seem severe, but it must have been necessary for the plan of God to be completed. To the average observer, it seems harsh and cruel. To the one understanding the things of the spiritual realm, it is very logical and reasonable.

Abraham (or Abram as he was then known) lived in the land of the East. That area is known for its occult activities and for origins of the horoscope and astrology that carries on even today. God certainly wanted to break the spiritual ties to other gods, and a change in location would help do that.

If we trace the generations of Abraham through Laban, Lot, and others, we can see a very selfish and materialistic family influence. The kind of life that God wanted to create in Abraham would have been hindered greatly by the spiritual seeds the family would have continually sown into him.

For God to have the kind of man he wanted in Abraham, a clean break was needed. He needed to be out there all alone. He needed to call upon the Lord on a regular basis. God needed to become a major influence and the primary sower of seed into the person of Abraham. So, God called him out, away from his family. Incidentally, it was not until after Abraham separated from Lot that the blessing of the son of the promise came!

In Genesis 18:19, God reveals His purpose in choosing Abraham:

> For I have known him, in order that he may command his children and his household after him, that they keep the way of the LORD, to do

> righteousness and justice, that the LORD may
> bring to Abraham what He has spoken to him.

God desires for parents to be a godly spiritual influence. He chose Abraham because He had found in him a man that He knew would exert the right kind of influence on the generations. But there had to be a clean break. The influence of the other generations, of relatives, had to be cut off. Why? Because family has a two-sided influence on our person.

From our family, we draw a spiritual heritage. We understand that we have a genetic heritage from our parents, but what we don't understand is that we also have a spiritual heritage. Exodus 20 tells us that the sins of the parents will be passed on to the third and the fourth generation. It doesn't say that the punishment is passed on, it says that the sin is passed on. As a parent, my sin nature is passed on as seed that is lying dormant within the spiritual makeup of my children. If a time of abundance comes for my child, it will likely manifest.

God is not using this to cruelly judge His people. He created us so that we might pass on a righteous heritage to our children. Unfortunately, the same law allows us to pass on an unrighteous heritage. Abraham had a spiritual heritage from his family. If he had stayed in the land, the time of abundance would have likely overtaken him, grown to weed stage, bearing more bad spiritual seed, and then seeding his spirit with even more negative stuff that he would have had to contend with. Another time of abundance of negative stuff would have been much more likely, producing even more seed.

God wants us to pass on a righteous heritage to our children. Proverbs 22:1a tells us that, "A good name is to be chosen rather than great riches." The word "name" here is all about heritage. It is about character. It is about spiritual seed sown into me because of whom I belong to. It is about receiving a righteous heritage. Why? Because if I inherit great riches and don't have the right stuff on the inside, I will just squander it. On the other hand, if I inherit no money, but have the right stuff on the inside, I will end up with great riches.

My Part in the "Sowing"

The key is beginning to see what is really inside me. One source of what is inside me is my heritage. A second source is my experiences. People and situations are constantly sowing in to "me", into my person, or my spirit. What they sow is somewhat unavoidable and yet somewhat controllable. First, I can leave. Like Abraham, I can change my circumstances. I can change what is being sown into me experientially. That can bring a major change.

Second, I can monitor and interpret what comes into my person. If someone makes a snide remark to me, I can interpret it as, "That person really doesn't like me." Or "He is really stressed out lately." Or " He sure uses a lot of sarcasm to try to communicate." In the end, my interpretation has everything to do with the seed that will end up being sown in me. I could get down, hateful, sympathetic, or even joyful from a single comment spoken by the same person in the same way.

Often, a change in surroundings does absolutely no good because of the way we interpret events. Some people actually move halfway around the world trying to get away from their problems. Unfortunately, they carry their inner stuff with them. And if a part of their inner stuff is to interpret life with a chip on their shoulder, their problems will return almost immediately. A change in scenery will change nothing.

That wasn't true for Abraham. God had found in him a man that would respond to Him and who would pass on that righteous response to his children, both as a heritage and as an experience. God led Abraham out and tested him over and over again. He even asked Abraham to sacrifice his son of the promise, Isaac. Each time, Abraham acknowledged that what God wanted was more important than what he wanted. A righteous heritage was in the making.

Creating a Righteous Heritage

That is one of God's most precious goals for each one of us: to develop a righteous heritage within each of us. The actual behavior that is showing up at any given moment is really secondary to the overall heritage that God is trying to develop within us over the long haul. I believe that at times God is willing to put up with some external behaviors that He doesn't like, as long as a person's inner makeup is being changed in the right way.

Abraham, at one point, passed off his wife as his sister. This is not, nor was it an admirable action. Unfortunately, he created a heritage when he did it and his son Isaac repeated the exact same sin with his wife years later and even with the very same person, King Abimelech. It is important to note that Isaac was not even born when Abraham slighted Sarah, nor was Abraham still alive when Isaac passed off Rebekah as his sister. Despite not having any direct experiential connection, the spiritual heritage influence was strong enough to help recreate the exact same sin.

Even so, God honored both Abraham and Isaac by protecting their wives from the foreign kings and even causing the kings to give them gifts instead of punishing them. Why was God so generous? Because in each case the men were in a dependence relationship with God and were learning that they could trust Him to take care of them. Through their own foolishness and through the kings, God was able to teach them more about trust. And they each received at least a mild rebuke for their folly as well.

Choosing Real Change

So why can't I change? We can't change because all we want to change is behavior. God wants to change us. He wants to develop a righteous heritage in us. Sometimes, the cost of that is very high. In fact, Jesus says that to receive not just a good heritage, but His heritage, we must "take up our cross daily" and die to all of our selfish wants totally. For some, that may call for a radical change in location. For others, relationships must end. For others, a way of thinking must be stopped. For others, there is great financial sacrifice. For all, there must be death to self.

So why can't I change? We can and do all the time. The only question is how are we changing. Are we changing toward His heritage or one of our own choosing? Or is the world simply molding and changing us almost beyond our control? God is waiting for each one of us. His heritage is freely available through the death of His Son. He is waiting to adopt us and give us a new heritage. He is waiting to spend time with each one of us and to give us new experiences. So what are we waiting for? Get the right stuff! The change is coming on the inside, today invisible but one day for all to see!

Chapter Twelve

The Greatest Changes

The greatest changes are never seen, because they take place in our invisible part. Changes are brought on by events, people, or even simple decisions. Some people make seemingly radical shifts in behavior. Often the radical shifts are not so radical if you can get beneath the exterior. Generally, seemingly radical changes have been building over a period of time in the form of significant changes on the inside. Most often, these changes go unnoticed.

Perhaps no event affected the United States like the Great Depression. Certainly one could argue that the Revolutionary War or the Civil War had a far greater impact. Yet, each of these wars was a culmination of tensions that had been building for almost a century or even longer. The outward battle was almost an inevitable result of the inward differences that were building at the time.

The Great Depression and the corresponding scarcity of World War II was different. An entire generation of people seemed to respond to a happening in a common manner that would affect the destiny of the nation for years to come. Instead of inner tensions resulting in a major event, this time a major happening wrote on the hearts of scores of Americans.

Between the war and the depression, many Americans endured a time of having to do without the normal luxuries and even many necessities. In response to this time of lack, there seemed to be a collective vow in the hearts of many Americans saying, "Whatever it takes, we will never pass this way again."

For some, that vow took the form of working longer hours to build up a reserve. Others used an incredibly frugal lifestyle as a hedge. Most began to set their sights on providing a "better" life for their children. Still others began to turn to government programs as a future hope. Mostly, materialistic concerns came to the forefront. Scarcity and lack had made an indelible mark on the hearts of a generation.

Quality of life quickly became measured in terms of material comforts. Accelerated by some of the technological advancements, a preoccupation with "things" and "modern comforts" became more and more important on the inner-scale of values. The hearts of a nation were collectively changing. The day would soon come when teenagers would kill in cold blood simply to get a pair of sneakers with the right name on the side.

For others, the Great Depression provided a backdrop of the faithfulness of God. Testimony after testimony can be found of God providing in unusual or miraculous ways. These hearts too, were changed by this time. They were changed more toward loyalty to God. Material things became less valuable. For them, possessions came and went, but God abided with them continually.

One event. Two drastically different endings. The difference is what was written on the heart. The hearts of one group were changed more toward materialism and dependence on self or government. The hearts of the other group grew stronger in the Lord. Both were changing. Little of the change was visible.

Good "Sin" and Bad "Righteousness"

One person smokes. One person doesn't. By legalistic standards, one is holy and one is not. But God has a very different point of view. Certainly, smoking is harmful to the body and is not something that God condones as it does destroy the temple of God. Yet, there is much more to the picture than a simple black and white drawing.

The person responding to the Great Depression with frugality can hardly be cited for doing anything morally wrong. Yet, if the frugality is a way to avoid depending on God, or if it elevates the accumulation of material things to a status more important than God, it is a sin. It is tremendously damaging to the heart. Because of its "good" side, the evil being written on the heart may take years, even generations to manifest, but it will show up sooner or later.

In the same way, some people have been able, by a sheer act of the will, to quit smoking. A strong person can take control of his or her life and rule over many of the negatives that are traditional "sins." Again, the end result is usually an independence from God, with a harsh judgment toward "weaker" men who cannot live up to similar standards. The person then exalts his own lifestyle of good works and considers himself righteous. The fruit of this life will also soon manifest itself, showing the ugliness that it holds, often in the next generation.

Both the frugal person and the one who quits smoking appear to be the godly ones of their generation. Many times, because of a strong will, that appearance is maintained throughout their entire lives. Yet, "for some unknown reason," their children seem to have no interest in God. The children display, in an even stronger way, the dependence on self and refuse the veneer of Christianity that their parents chose. For the children, self-reliance is simply taken one more step and God is an unnecessary nuisance.

In contrast, the smoker who truly has a heart for God is often very broken and contrite before God and man. Ongoing efforts to quit have brought a sense of helplessness, and a knowledge of the need to depend totally on God if the goal of quitting smoking is ever to be realized. What is being written on this person's heart is a meekness and a humility that will also manifest itself one day in victory over the habit, as well as a hunger for God in the next generation. The immediate outward picture does not tell the whole story. What God is doing in the heart is the MOST significant change.

I do not give this example to give people a license to sin. The only reason good could come out of the situation is because of the repentant heart that was learning the need to be dependent on God. There is a big difference between someone struggling with an area of sin and the person who is willfully sinning.

Any willful sin writes ugly and grotesque things on the heart. It hardens the heart toward man and toward God. Unless God has a greater objective, like crushing a person's pride and independence, deliverance from sin should generally be expected on an immediate or at least a steadily improving basis. But, God has His order of priority. We prefer to be delivered of the visible sins first so that we will look good around fellow Christians. Sometimes God has other ideas.

A time of lack, like the Great Depression, is a signal from God that it is time to draw closer to Him and to depend even more than before. Unfortunately, some move away from Him, judging Him to be incapable of providing for their needs. They choose self instead.

Asa's Achieved Righteousness

King Asa is a perfect illustration of both drawing near to God and then later depending on self. In his early years, he came up against the million man army of the Ethiopians. Asa cried out to God for help (2 Chron. 14) and God answered.

On the one hand, Asa was God's man as he cleansed the land of idols and even removed Maachah, the Queen mother, because of her involvement in idolatry. Yet, at the same time, he set about the business of rebuilding the walls of all the towns and of accumulating wealth. Then in the thirty-fifth year of his reign, when King Baasha came against him, Asa took the silver and gold out of the Lord's house to try to buy protection from a foreign army. God rebuked him for his stupidity.

Later, Asa became diseased in his feet. The passage says that "in his disease he did not seek the Lord, but the physicians" (2 Chron. 16:12b). Through the prophet, God had already told Asa, "For the eyes of the Lord run to and fro throughout the whole earth, to show Himself strong on behalf of those whose heart is loyal to Him. In this you have done foolishly; therefore from now on you shall have wars" (2 Chron. 16:9). A time of difficulty is a signal to draw near to God, not to depend on self.

Because Asa had depended on his own wealth and had even stolen the monies from the treasuries of the temple to try to buy his way out of war danger, God rebuked Asa. And being the just God that He is, the sentence for trying to avoid war through the strength of man is to get more wars. Proverbs puts it this way: "The fear of the wicked will come upon him, and the desire of the righteous will be granted" (Prov. 10:24).

God, who deals primarily with the heart, allows the natural course of events to simply come to pass. The one who fears war will, through his focus, help bring that very war to pass. Faith is a spiritual force that works whether it is faith in God or faith in the evil to come. Faith in the evil coming to get me is called fear.

King Asa, after the war with the Ethiopians, spent the major part of his years fortifying the land so that, in the case of war, the nation would be ready. In itself, being prepared is not wrong. But I have to wonder if King Asa did not make an "I will never pass this way again" sort of vow. Being hung out by a thread with "only God" to depend on had been an unpleasant experience. Even though God had delivered Israel, for Asa it appears that a fear of war and a self-reliance had been established in his heart.

For years, these inner changes seemed to manifest in good ways. Asa strengthened the land and prospered. He cleansed the land of idols and the things that God hates. Yet even the cleansing of the land may have been a sign of his reliance on his own good works, rather than of a heart loyal to God. If indeed he was growing in loyalty to God, why was the latter part of his life such a radical departure from that same loyalty?

In Jeremiah, God asks the question "Can the Ethiopian change his skin or the leopard its spots? Then may you also do good who are accustomed to do evil" (Jer. 13:23). In Isaiah 28:10, God tells us that righteousness is "precept upon precept" and "line upon line." Asa certainly could have started out good and pure in his service of the Lord. However, the evil at the end of his life did not simply appear in a day.

If he started with a loyal heart, at some point something in his life shifted and he became "accustomed to do evil" and he was sowing "line upon line" toward evil. A single event (the war with Baasha) brought about a seemingly sudden change, but more than likely, that event was not the beginning of his turning away from God. Seeds of the negative change had been sown in his heart over a period of time.

In the end, the Scriptures make it very clear that Asa's good had turned to evil. He persecuted the prophets that tried to correct him and even mistreated others because of his rage (2 Chron. 16:10). He refused to turn to God in a time of war and he refused to turn to God in a time of sickness.

If indeed Asa's heart said, "I will never pass this way again," as a response to the Ethiopian war, his actions begin to make sense. His continuing "cleansing of the land" also fits if it is the heart of a person fortifying his position with God instead of being that of a person humbling himself and becoming continually more dependent upon God. The "fortified" person has a sense that God "owes" him. The humble person awaits more grace.

Righteous "Among Men"

Job can be seen in a similar way. In the beginning of the book, Job is a "fortified" righteous man. He even tries to extend his "fortification" to his children by sacrificing for them. It is almost a mentality of trying to ward off evil spirits through proper behavior and through sacrifice. If you listen to the complaints of Job throughout the long discourses of the book, that mentality of Job becomes obvious.

Some of the most "righteous" people are righteous for all the wrong reasons. True righteousness manifests itself in a humility and dependence before God. A false righteousness says "I deserve protection and a reward from God." True righteousness does not fear because it knows the God it serves is loving and kind. False righteousness goes to exaggerated lengths to "get it right" lest God punish me.

Often, the most righteous people really aren't righteous at all. They are "righteous among men," but God wants someone who is righteous before Him and not someone who is righteous compared to other men. The one who is righteous before Him is the one who depends on the righteousness of Christ for his strength and not on his own works.

If Asa really had been growing in love and loyalty to God throughout his life, his actions at the end of his life would have been much different. If Job really had begun with a humble heart, his discourse would have been much different and he would not have needed to totally humble himself, declaring himself to be "vile" (Job 40:4) after seeing some of the glory of God. Righteous works can be deceptive. A righteous heart is not deceived. It knows that it is not, nor can it ever be righteous in and of itself. It is only righteous because of what God has done. And it will never attempt to move out of that place of total dependence.

Going for the Greatest Changes

I fear that as a nation we missed it in the Great Depression. There is much evidence that we collectively moved from God-reliance to self-reliance. The popular phrase "God helps those that help themselves" is but one illustration of a subtle shift in understanding that is deadly. A move toward more education, accumulation of wealth, and a dependence on science and government to solve our problems are further evidences. No longer do we declare days of fasting and prayer as President Lincoln did in his days of crisis. No, we have become too advanced for that.

Education is not wrong. Wealth is not evil. Government is necessary, and science gives us understanding of God's creation. But when any of these areas begin to occupy a level of importance that only God should have, it is deadly.

What began in one generation as seemingly "changes for the better," I believe was truly manifested in the 1960's. Prayer was taken out of the schools, the Bible was banned, and the riots and rejection of authority began. In reality, it may have been nothing more than a visible reflection of the rejection of God that had begun in the hearts of the previous generation.

The greatest changes are never seen. They are subtle and hidden, at times, for generations. We live in a society that wants instant and immediate impact. God is a God of the forever. He is a God of the heart. The immediate is not nearly so important to Him. This fleshly man will soon decay and pass away. Our works will soon be forgotten. But our souls will live on in heaven forever.

He is the God of our hearts. The greatest changes are the invisible changes of the heart. And if it takes it years to come to fruition, that is not a problem for God. He wants our hearts. We want to look good. We want results. We want to be secure. He wants our hearts. He doesn't just want our works. He wants our hearts. Are you in the place of dependence today? The greatest change begins in an invisible way as we abide in Him.

Chapter Thirteen

The Transplant

We understand heart transplants. We understand clogged arteries and a blood flow that is shut down. No heart function means death. A restricted or stopped blood flow to a part of the body is a stroke that can cause paralysis or even a kind of "death" to an area of the body. Why can't we also understand the need for a constant flow of God's Spirit in, through, and around us in order for us to be spiritually alive?

No Spirit flow means spiritual death. A spiritual heart transplant is needed. Restricted spiritual flow brings spiritual paralysis and partial death. Spiritual cleansing is needed. God created us to need His flow constantly in the very same way that we need the flow of blood to every part of our body every minute of the day.

Ezekiel and Jeremiah both described a new "heart" that would come for God's people. In that day God says, "I will give you a new heart and put a new spirit within you; I will take the heart of stone out of your flesh and give you a heart of flesh. I will put My Spirit within you and cause you to walk in My statutes, and you will keep My judgments and do them" (Ezekiel 36:26-27). The people's hearts had grown cold. They were described as hearts of stone and not flesh. They needed a transplant! They had changed to the point that they were no longer a reflection of the living God, but more like a piece of dead, hard earth.

Removing the Hardness

In the parable of the sower and the seed, Jesus also is talking about the condition of the hearts of the people. With each of the kinds of soil, the sower is the same. And the seed is the same. It is God that is symbolically at work, sowing seed into these hearts. Yet, only one of the soils produces a crop. The other three are like Ezekiel's heart of stone. They do not have what it takes to be a reflection of the glory of God.

In this parable, there are four levels of "hardness" of soil (or symbolically of a heart) described. The first level is that of the "wayside" which represents the well-traveled path. Nothing is necessarily wrong with the soil (or the heart itself) except that the people spill over from the path to walk on this ground, leaving it hard.

The second type of soil is full of stones. It is inherently hard. It needs no one to walk on it. It is hard by nature. It has not been made hard. It is hard. In and of itself, it never will produce a good harvest.

The third kind of soil appears to be fertile soil. It is not hardened by life, and it is not stony. If we were to compare this kind of soil to a physical heart, it would be a heart that is strong. This soil has all the nutrients to produce a good crop. In the same way, many times a person's heartbeat is strong, able to produce a good flow of blood. But there is a problem. The blood flow is restricted by clogged arteries, and it is as if the person had a weak or hardened heart. The crop of this soil is restricted by the weeds. The cares of this life distract the heart and it is no longer fruitful.

The fourth type of heart is one to rejoice over. It bears fruit 30, 60, and 100 times over. It produces what the farmer hopes it will produce. It responds to God. And the response to God is not like the other soils where a single seed is lost. Instead, at the bare minimum, 29 seeds are gained. This one soil, this one heart, more than makes up for the seeds that are lost.

So it is in God's kingdom, one man responding to God produces incredible amounts of fruit from one seed, more than enough to eclipse all the seeds that are wasted on the hard hearts. One man living empowered by the Spirit of God more than makes up for the many who try to imitate the goodness of God through human effort.

Yet, it is not so much the soils that are different as it is the care of the soils that is different. For soil to be fruitful, it cannot be packed down from travels of this life. Year after year, the soil must be plowed to keep it loose. Otherwise, it will become good for nothing.

It is our job, with the aid of the Holy Spirit to plow up our soil, to keep our hearts soft and usable. If we stay in touch with the Spirit, He will bring to our minds those things that are hindering our walk with the Lord. If we respond in repentance and with obedience, the soil becomes usable.

We tend to be creatures of habit. Some of those habits are necessary, but many can create a hardness of heart that resists the Spirit of God. Many times, even the best of habits, ones that God commands, can become so ritualistic that the Spirit has absolutely no chance to influence them any more. The habit has become its own automatic pilot activity. The Spirit's influence is no longer allowed. That is the soil of the well traveled path.

To produce fruit, the soil must also be kept free from stones. One might think that clearing the stones from a field is a "one time" event. That would be nice, but it is not so. If there are stones on the surface, there are probably stones beneath the surface. Once the stones at the surface are cleared, the supple soil will begin to settle down and pack in around the stones beneath the surface. Before long, a pressure underneath the stones develops, and the stones are then forced to the surface. The field may have been completely cleaned last year, but the ground once again is stony and in need of cleansing.

Our spiritual soil is no different. When born again, a new believer appears to have all the stones removed. It would seem that the soil is absolutely ready to produce a great harvest, year after year. Unfortunately, stones do work their way back to the surface!

The same is certainly true of the weedy soil. Weeds beget more weeds. A few weeds this year means a whole host of weeds next year. The only recourse is a constant and vigilant care over a period of years.

Sin begets more sin. One lie spins into a dozen more. A lifestyle results. The heart begins to change more and more into an image that no longer reflects the image of Christ that once seemed to be present.

And what about the good soil? Is it just naturally good? Perhaps it started with an advantage, but even good soil can easily become packed if you put a path through it. And at times stones can work to the surface and weeds certainly love to grow in good soil. The good soil is not good because it is inherently different. It is good because it is kept that way with proper care. The farmer gives it the kind of care that is essential for a good crop. It is plowed; it is cleaned of any debris; it is kept free of weeds; and it is fertilized.

Our hearts are no different. Life will make them hard. Stones will surface. Weeds will grow. We need the constant flow of the Spirit to remain fruitful. It is the Spirit's ongoing care of the heart that makes the difference!

What Begins in the Spirit . . .

Seeing a person who is born again, we recognize what Ezekiel is saying. God does take out a heart of stone and put in a heart of flesh. Through our confession and our prayers we open the door for God to impart to us a new nature. We realize that the person that goes to the altar for prayer is not the same person that returns from prayer. The person who is born again is a "new creature" (2 Cor. 5:17). He has a new heart.

What we often don't accept is that the soil needs plowing, cleaning, and weeding on an ongoing basis. One of the laws of nature is that the field that is not kept up will return to an unusable state. And how is the field first cleansed? By the Spirit of God. And how is it kept as fertile soil? Certainly not through our own efforts. Paul says it this way:

> O foolish Galatians! Who has bewitched you that
> you should not obey the truth, before whose eyes
> Jesus Christ was clearly portrayed among you as
> crucified? This only I want to learn from you: Did
> you receive the Spirit by the works of the law, or

> by the hearing of faith? Are you so foolish?
> Having begun in the Spirit, are you now being
> made perfect by the flesh? (Gal 3:1-3).

We understand that we must be born again by the Spirit of God. Yet we think that we can continue our walk now without the Spirit of God. We think that our cleansing is once for all time. We believe that we have received an impartation from God that will take care of everything forever.

When Paul chides them for returning to "the works of the law," I believe it is comparable to the person who is born again and then tries to live the Christian life in his own strength. We try to be "good for God." In reality, a field once cleansed will return to rocks if not tended. A human heart dies in minutes without a life-giving flow of oxygen through it. Likewise, the new fleshly heart that God gives soon becomes hard if it is not continually kept soft by the flow of His Spirit. We are commanded to "obey the truth" (Gal. 3:1), but we are only able to do that with an ongoing flow of His Spirit.

A Spiritual Beginning

Many times, people have a hard time "continuing" in the Spirit, because they are taught a "fleshly" beginning to the spiritual life. Romans 8:16 says that, "The Spirit Himself bears witness with our spirit that we are children of God."

The beginning of our new life in Christ should be a spiritual experience. We should understand what it means for "God's Spirit to bear witness with our spirit." Instead, many times people only make contact with what another person says. The "convert" hears a formula, repeats a prayer, and then is told that he is born again. There is a mental assent on the part of the "convert" but no real contact between God and the person is established.

The Scriptures clearly teach (1 Cor. 6:17-20) that when we are born again, we are reunited with God. His Spirit begins to interact freely with our spirits. We feel the resulting release as a peace in our own spirits. There is a newness, a freshness, a sense of having a new heart that really is made of flesh and not stone. There is a sense of joy and a desire to celebrate the fullness and richness of life that God has given to us. This is beginning in the Spirit.

How can a person who does not even begin with any sense of the Spirit continue in the Spirit? If we reduce the born again experience to a formula and a response that we request them to follow, their chance of connecting with the Spirit is much more limited. If we are not careful, we become the focal point and the person ends up trying to respond to our requests instead of having a relationship with the Lord. From the beginning, we need to try to get them focused on what the Spirit is doing in them.

We need to teach them about receiving an impartation from the Spirit. Every believer should have a Romans 8:16 impartation experience, sensing the Spirit's adoption and the glorious feeling of "I truly am a child of God. Abba Father!" For those who begin with a clear sense of the Spirit's presence, continuing in the Spirit is normal and natural. Otherwise, walking the "best we know how" is about all that we can do.

Even with a strong spiritual beginning, the normal human condition is for the heart to harden. How often I have heard statements like "Oh if I could just get back to what it was like

when . . .!" The point of God's impartation to us is a high point
. . . or perhaps a kind of a low point if God is about the business
of discipline. Yet even in discipline, we sense His love and there
is a therapeutic cleansing that leaves us refreshed in spirit. If a
believer goes for years without an impartation, the condition of
the soil is guaranteed to be full of stones and weeds and will be
very packed down. There will be no spiritual fruit.

Being born again should not be an experience that we point back
to, but a lifestyle that we live. The flow of blood must be
constant. Any restriction of the blood flow results in stroke or
death. The flow of the Spirit must be constant. Any restriction
results in spiritual hardness and in spiritual death.

Several times, Paul refers to prayer without ceasing. He is not
talking about the mental exercise of prayer. At times, our minds
are and must be occupied with other things. He is not talking
about quitting all of life to go into a prayer closet and never eat
or sleep. He is talking about a constant flow of the Spirit.
Prayer is communion with God. It is a subconscious awareness
of His presence that never leaves us nor forsakes us.

For most, that is a fairy tale. The presence of God is at best
fleeting. The right church situation is hoped for to make the
difference. Or perhaps, all hope is lost and like the "bewitched
Galatians," life becomes nothing more than a walking out of the
best that the flesh can do.

Coming Under the Presence

The presence of God is our life blood. It is not negotiable. Or
should I say our awareness of the presence of God is not
negotiable. He is always everywhere present. It is not His

presence that changes. It is our awareness of His presence.
Even more accurately, it is our submission to His influence in
our lives that allows Him to be "more" present in our lives.

John describes the different presences of God:

> And I will pray the Father, and He will give you
> another Helper, that He may abide with you
> forever– the Spirit of truth, whom the world
> cannot receive, because it neither sees Him nor
> knows Him; but you know Him, for He dwells
> with you and will be in you" (John 14:16-17).

On the one hand, the world, or those that are not God's
children, are described as not being able to see or sense the
Spirit. John 6:44 clarifies that even a non-believer can be drawn
by the Spirit, as no person can even come to Christ unless He
draws that person to Himself. Yet, this drawing must be done
almost completely apart from the senses and the understanding
of the unbeliever as spiritual things must be "spiritually
discerned" (1 Cor. 2:14b). The Spirit is "with" the unbeliever in
that He is present and watching, but from the outside.

In John 14:16-17, the disciples are described as having the Spirit
"with" them. This could refer to the fact that Jesus is with them
and accordingly there is a special presence of the Spirit because
of Jesus. However, these are the very same disciples who had
been commissioned to go out to heal the sick, to cast out
demons, and to minister to the people. Could they have done
this apart from the power of the Spirit?

The Spirit was obviously more "with" those disciples than He
was "with" an unbeliever. There was a power upon them that
far exceeded that of the regular person. Even so, Jesus said that

the Spirit was "with" them and would be "in" them. There was an even closer relationship of the Spirit that was yet to come.

On the day of Pentecost, in Acts 2, that day arrived. Those in the upper room were "baptized" with the Holy Spirit and with fire. Both Jesus and John had spoken of this day. It was the beginning of a special intimacy that the Holy Spirit could have with each and every believer with the result of having a greater power to live a holy life and to minister to others.

The word "baptism" speaks of an immersion. If a person is immersed in water, he is placed under the water until every part of him is wet. The water sticks to every part of his body.   In the same way, these people who were baptized in the Holy Spirit were completely immersed. The Spirit has a new freedom to flow in and to stick to every part of their lives. There is a surrender on the part of the people and a filling on the part of the Spirit. The Spirit is now "in" them and not just "with" them.

The key to all of the spiritual walk is a Spirit flow in our lives. Many people that I talk to today have no sense of having a spiritual part and have little understanding of the Spirit's flow in their lives. Many are like the disciples of Acts 19 who declared that " we have not so much as heard whether there is a Holy Spirit" (v. 2b). Having been taught to follow after a prescribed manner of action, many are missing the most precious part of the Christian walk.

We need an impartation from God daily, even on a minute by minute basis. Many have been taught to be satisfied with a one-time impartation at the time of being born again. That would be like getting a new heart and then immediately shutting off the blood flow. We are born again in order to have a relationship with our heavenly Father. We are given a new heart that can feel the things that He feels and understand the things that He understands. Why would we want to throw all that away and just "live a good life"?

The key to producing fruit is the soil of our own hearts. The key to having good soil is the cleansing and nurturing work of the Holy Spirit. Self effort won't get the job done! We need the constant impartation that the Spirit will give us if we will only seek His control for our lives. Let us not be like the foolish Galatians who returned to the arm of the flesh, but let us prepare our hearts to go on in the Spirit!

Chapter Fourteen

Starting the Flow

Receiving from God is a strange mixture of preparation of self and making oneself available to God, while at the same time recognizing that self effort will do little or nothing. Unless God pours Himself out upon us, all of our efforts are as nothing in moving us toward any real life of righteousness.

It is important to understand from the beginning that He is God. No amount of movement on our part can guarantee His coming to us. Isaiah 58 describes a nation that was "seeking" the Lord through fasting and prayer. The last part of verse two says, "They ask of Me the ordinances of justice; they take delight in approaching God." These people were very active and God seemingly should have responded. Instead, the first part of the verse completes the picture: "Yet they seek Me daily, And delight to know My ways, as a nation that did righteousness, and did not forsake the ordinance of their God."

The people of Israel were trying to force the hand of God to move on their behalf. Certainly, they were missing the main ingredient, a humble heart that desired to walk in righteousness. They though that through their religious activity they could make God intervene. They were wrong. In fact, if anything, they were increasing the wrath of God and not currying favor.

God does promise to respond to a humble and contrite heart, but what activity can we do to "prove" our humility? And who is to say that we are not deceiving ourselves with religious activity the same way the Israelites were in Isaiah 58? At times, it is our movement that hinders His coming. He wants us to realize that it is indeed His moving that makes the difference. If a believer has just climbed a "high mountain," the believer is likely to think that it is his own climbing that has made the difference.

Often it is indeed a quieting of self that actually releases God to move. Yet, at times, it is even a headlong binge into sin that precedes God's moving. There is no hard and fast rule that absolutely guarantees His moving. If there were, human effort could "force" the hand of God and "guarantee" a spiritual change. Man could then get the credit and share the glory for the change with God.

God's moving comes as grace (Eph. 2:8). One of the meanings of the word "grace" is "gift." A gift is a gift. If something is given in response to a work done, it is a payment. To be a true gift, the moving of God must come first with the response of the believer second. The response of faith (Eph. 2:8) is needed, but it is a response just as thankfulness would be a response to receiving a gift.

Our coming to God really is a response to His moving. The only problem is that we somehow miss His part and are very aware of our part. At times, it can be even humorous watching believers try to force the hand of God to move by doing the same things that were done just before He moved the last time. Some will kneel crying out with great tears. Others will sing and shout praises. When no answer comes, the "magical, make God move" behavior simply becomes more and more exaggerated. They think that it was their actions preceding the move of God that made the difference the last time. So why won't it work again?

God is God. He is the One that deserves the credit. He deserves to be the center. He deserves the glory. The feeble efforts of man do not compare with what God has done in Christ, and they are not worthy to share in His glory. He takes the initiative. He starts the process. Because God is God, He is able and does at times move on the hardest of hearts in ways that defy logic, reminding us that He will move when and how He chooses. It truly is God that makes the difference. We are important to Him which makes our efforts important to Him. But He is and will remain, God.

Our Part

Even so, the "initiative" of man (which may actually be more of a response to a hidden moving of God) does not go unnoticed by God. God has committed Himself to move on behalf of the humble (James 4:6), the spiritually hungry (Matt. 5:6), and those that call on His name (Rom. 10:13).

Our attitude should not be one of helplessly waiting around for God to move. James 4:6-10 says:

> But He gives more grace. Therefore He says: 'God resists the proud, but gives grace to the humble.' Therefore submit to God. Resist the devil and he will flee from you. Draw near to God and He will draw near to you. Cleanse your hands, you sinners; and purify your hearts, you double-minded. Lament and mourn and weep!

> Let your laughter be turned to mourning and
> your joy to gloom. Humble yourselves in the
> sight of the Lord, and He will lift you up.

This passage is full of things that the believer can do to begin to open the flow of the Spirit in his life. Perhaps the greatest is God's promise to give grace or a "gift" to the humble. The grace of God has two parts. On the one hand is the gift of forgiveness that leaves us clean and able to freely interact with God, just as if we had never sinned. On the other hand is the gift of enablement that is needed to meet each and every situation we encounter in life with the authority of a true child of God. If we can humble ourselves, the likelihood of the flow of God's Spirit in and through us has greatly increased.

And how do we humble ourselves? The passage in James gives us an extended definition of humility. The first requirement is submission to God. If we could truly pass this test, there would be no need for God to withhold Himself at times. Yet, even as was made clear in earlier chapters, we deceive ourselves and think ourselves to be submitted when we are not. We must be tested and proved. He does not always pour Himself out at the first sign of submission, but often allows a testing time to do its work of slowly marinating the attitude of submission into us over a period of time.

It may be a surprise that the very next sentence is to "Resist the devil and he will flee from you." Submission seems like a kind of soft surrender that is not compatible with resisting the devil. In reality, a submission to God is an active subduing of the flesh that will be met with violent spiritual warfare from the enemy. There is nothing Satan fears more than a submitted Christian. Satan will do everything in his power to thwart true submission.

When the believer begins to say, "My body is Yours to use Lord," and "Your will for my life is what I choose to do," the battle has begun. Especially if the believer moves out of the passive mode and begins to actively seek the will of God for his life, Satan will come out fighting. Many lose it at this point. They are distracted by the battles. The difficulties are, to them, a sign that they are doing something wrong. Instead, difficulties may mean that we are doing something right. It may mean that it is simply time to resist the devil and to watch him flee.

The Power of Focus

Submission takes absolute concentration. The focus of the believer must be unbroken. Troubles often break down the focus of the believer. A believer that is divided in focus can be defeated by the devil. A believer that is singly focused on God will not be defeated but will be able to resist the devil.

This leads perfectly into the next line: "draw near to God and He will draw near to you." Though nothing on our part absolutely guarantees a specific response from God, this line gives us hope. If we can simply "draw near to God" then He will "draw near" to us. So how do we do that? It goes back to focus, meditation, time, and attention.

God calls us to worship Him "in spirit and in truth" (John 4:24). There is a part of our being that is called our spirit. That part of us is able to make contact with God and to give Him the kind of undivided focus that He is worthy of having. James refers to a kind of person that is unworthy of answered prayer. This man is "double-minded" and "unstable in all his ways" (James 1:8). He is not able to isolate his focus upon God.

Part of drawing near to God is learning to isolate our focus upon Him. Memorizing and meditating upon His Word is an excellent way to begin to do this. At first, these activities will be nearly impossible. Your spirit will be restless, and Satan will do everything he can to keep you distracted. You might even declare (if you haven't already) "I just can't memorize."

If we can focus, we can memorize and meditate. If we choose not to, it will be easy to declare ourselves as being incapable. Drawing near to God takes effort. It is essential for us to open up our spiritual part in a way that allows God to flow freely. He desires to move into a relationship that is not just "with" us, but one that is "in" us. But He cannot trust that kind of intimacy to one that is double-minded.

Not only is the double-minded person a bad risk for God, but he is like a clogged artery. He will not allow a free flow of the Spirit. Having a multiple focus is much like having multiple gods. The very first commandment is to have only one God, the Lord Most High. This kind of idolatry blocks the flow of God's Spirit in us. We might judge such a person to be "misguided" or "fearful" or even "cowardly", but the Scriptures calls him double-minded and unworthy of receiving of the things of God.

Drawing near to God comes down to focus. He will be just as close to us as we are focused on Him. We have that promise. He never fails in His promises. The battle will rage around us. Our submission will be tested. Our focus will be challenged, but if we can stay centered on the Lord, the battle is as good as won.

For those struggling (which is all of us), James offers further advice. "Cleanse your hands, you sinner; and purify your hearts, you double-minded." Which of us in our own strength can singly focus upon God? None that I know of can. Thus comes the true humbling. The hands and the hearts need cleansing. The standard lies beyond us.

It is time to "Lament and mourn and weep!" (James 4:9a). James continues saying, "Let your laughter be turned to mourning and your joy to gloom. Humble yourselves in the sight of the Lord, and He will lift you up" (v. 9b-10). When an undivided focus on God becomes our goal, it is easy to see how short of the mark we fall. True weeping is not far away. Real mourning will follow. We realize that the prospect of God's presence is but a distant promise, due to the mixed up nature of our own hearts.

Repentance is deep and honest. A seeing of self brings humility that cannot be feigned. It is not hollow, but is based in a knowledge of the truth. This completes the "worship in spirit and in truth." The humility of recognizing who we are and Who God is opens a spiritual flow. It allows God to lift us up as only the flow of His Spirit can. When our spirit is open to God in this way, His flow can be expected and should be normal. There may be times and seasons during which He draws back in order to cause us to seek Him out all the more, but the humble man can generally expect His presence.

Bringing it Together: God's Part and Our Part

"Draw near to God." "Humble yourselves." God commands it. It can be done. At least it can be done with His help. Perhaps that is the clincher. The man who thinks he can do it will never get to his destination of being close to God. The one who recognizes, a few steps into the journey, his desperate need for help, will likely make it all the way there. We make ourselves available. We do our best to focus. We begin to see enough truth to bring true repentance and humility. God does the rest.

This is a "formula" for the flow of God. It is called utter dependence or absolute and active submission. No passive "whatever" will work here. It is a headlong pursuit of making God's agenda our agenda. It involves the daily disciplines of Bible study, memorization, prayer, and fasting. It means a giving of self to others in need just as Christ would have done. It is a steady pursuit of God over a prolonged period of time. Being single-minded is the key. Nothing less will do.

The norm for today is multi-tasking. The productive person can handle two, three, or even more tasks at once. To change from a multi-tasking norm to a God-only focus is not an easy thing. In fact, it will feel uncomfortable because it is not productive. It does not seem to be "taking care of the details." It seems to be "irresponsible" and a "poor use of talents."

God did not ask us to be a bunch of busy beavers. He even tells His disciples "For you have the poor with you always" (Matt. 26:11a). That was Jesus' way of saying the needs would never (this side of heaven) be completely taken care of through human effort. No matter how hard we work, the effects of the curse of sin will not be completely overcome.

God asks us to be His worshipers. Worship is about submission. It is about focus. It is about being wastefully lavish in what we give Him, even to the point of seeming foolishness. That is what the woman at Bethany did when she poured out a whole bottle of oil on Jesus. And it was expensive oil, worth a whole year's wages. It was lavish and foolish, except for one thing. Jesus was and is the Son of God. He was worth it. And He is worth it today.

Go ahead and be lavish. Be foolish even in your use of time that you give Him. Others will criticize, but it is a necessary step on your way toward being single-minded. Throw a party with Jesus as your only invited guest. Open the Scriptures and read. Sing songs to Him. Shout His praises. Rejoice in the gift of His salvation. Jump and clap like your team had just won the big game. Tell Him you love Him and be quiet and intimate for a season. Grab hold of His Word like that of a close lover and hide it deep in your heart. Journal your thoughts and feelings and any impressions that He gives you. What an evening! What a day! What a God to waste yourself upon! He is worth it. He is worthy.

Chapter Fifteen

The Mountaintops

I remember one of the first times I ever went skiing. The incredible majesty of the snow-covered mountains with the sun reflecting brilliantly was breathtaking. Even being a racing maniac anxious to get down the mountain, I just stopped to stare and to appreciate. It was a sight I will never forget.

There are spiritual mountaintops. They set the standard for spiritual experience. They are the breathtaking instances when we "know that we know" that the Spirit of God has really visited us. At other times, we may even doubt that we are a Christian, or we may think that God has really left us. But not on the mountaintop. For a few brief moments, the glory of Jesus transfigured is our experience, an experience never to be forgotten.

Moses' first recorded "mountaintop" experience was on the backside of a desert with a bush that was on fire but still did not burn. I do not believe that this was Moses' first experience with God. Stephen, sharing under the inspiration of the Holy Spirit, says of Moses, "For he supposed that his brethren would have understood that God would deliver them by his hand, but they did not understand" (Acts 7:25).

How did Moses get this understanding that he was to be the deliverer of Israel? Perhaps his mother had put that notion into his head during the earlier years as she nursed him. More than likely, the burning bush was not Moses' first spiritual experience. I believe that he had previously experienced a visitation from God that had changed him.

Hebrews tells us that Moses esteemed "the reproach of Christ greater riches than the treasures in Egypt, for he looked to the reward" (Heb. 11:26b). Moses made this choice forty years before the burning bush experience. How was Moses to know "the reward" in a vivid way if he had not experienced some taste of what heaven had to offer?

Turning Aside to God

Was Moses simply so much more spiritual than any man alive that hearing the stories of his ancestors, he just "knew" that he was the man to deliver Israel and that God would reward him for his troubles? Moses was a man just like we are. I believe that the mountaintop of God's presence had already paid Moses a visit. And like his ancestor Abraham, when God called, Moses answered.

When God called again at the burning bush, Moses, though still broken and hurting from his earlier failure, answered again. God takes up right where He left off, asking Moses to be the deliverer of His people. Moses responds as a broken man, thinking he has nothing to offer God.

Moses actually has much to offer God. Exodus 3:3 records, "Then Moses said, 'I will now turn aside and see this great sight, why the bush does not burn.' " The greatest question in the spiritual realm is "Where is your focus?" For most of us, the answer is on the things that matter to self. For Moses, his response indicates a curiosity about the things of God and His presence. Verse 4 says that, "So when the Lord saw that he turned aside to look, God called to him . . .." The very fact that Moses turned aside was important to God!

Often, the mountaintop experiences await us, if only we will turn aside for a moment to look. Most mountaintops come during a time of prayer or during a special season of focus upon God. Though this passage with Moses gives us no indication that he had been seeking God, throughout Moses' later life, he is a man that is constantly seeking more of the presence of God. It is not likely that this part of his person suddenly emerged because of one burning bush visitation. I believe Moses had a heart tender toward the Lord from the very beginning.

I have heard some say, "I have been a Christian for years and I have never had a vision or heard the voice of God or anything else supernatural." It is said in a way to indicate that this should be the normal experience for the believer. And, in fact, it was normal for the people in Moses' day. But I prefer Moses' experience of going deeper with God to that of the normal person. My heart is set on seeing the life of God released in and through me. I do not care to have a "normal" spiritual life!

Extraordinary Experience of an Extraordinary God

If the life of God is to be released in me, it will not be because I am an extraordinary person, but because I serve an extraordinary God. And it won't be just because I serve an extraordinary God. Many have served Him without walking with Him in any real depth. I can only respond in an extraordinary way if I have had an extraordinary experience of Him in me.

Ephesians 3:20-21 says, "Now to Him who is able to do exceedingly abundantly above all that we ask or think, according to the power that works in us, to Him be glory in the church by Christ Jesus to all generations, forever and ever. Amen." God can do incredible things through and to us only according to "the power that works in us." If we have a mundane and non-supernatural experience of God working in us, God is greatly limited.

In contrast, we can be open to and seeking for every fiber of our being to be filled with the Spirit of God in a supernatural power. Suddenly the potential for the power of God working toward and through us is greatly increased. "The power that works in us" sets the limit for His power to work whether His power is released in a small way or in great quantities.

It is also interesting to note that it is the "power that works in **us**." The Spirit of God needs each believer completely, but He also desires and needs all of us collectively. His fullness is only expressed when the Body, when all of us collectively, are open to Him and fully seeking Him. Then will His power be fully manifested.

In Acts 2, when the disciples had been waiting before the Lord in prayer and were in one accord, the Spirit came with an incredible "mountaintop" display. The description of His coming includes a rushing mighty wind, tongues of fire, and speaking in other tongues. Later in the chapter, Peter refers to visions, dreams, and prophecies as being a result of the coming of the Holy Spirit in fullness.

Virtually every spiritual mountaintop is, by its very definition, "supernatural." It happens first and foremost in the spiritual realm, the invisible realm. The totality of what has happened cannot be measured or seen by the naked eye. It cannot be proven to a bystander. What can be seen is the response of the person who has had the spiritual experience. Peter and his uneducated friends were suddenly very different. Moses returned to Egypt despite his previous failure.

At times, there is also a supernatural "sign" in the mind, emotions, or body of the person that has had the supernatural experience. Zacharias was struck dumb. Daniel was left weak and faint and emotionally shaken. Even Nebuchadnezzar was impacted in countenance from his divine dream. Today, many would classify these reactions as being of demonic origin simply because of their extreme nature.

Those who shut out the supernatural virtually tell God, "You are limited to working through my intellect and through human experiences." If we eliminate the supernatural, what will be the end result of "according to the power that works in us"? Is it any wonder that many of His churches are weak and without power? Is it any wonder that the American church is largely without new converts? As a nation, we are predisposed against the supernatural in our own individual lives.

A New Mode of Operation

It is time we change our mode of operation as a church. Being born again is a very clear and resounding spiritual miracle. It is the restoration of communion between the Spirit of God and a man or woman, boy or girl. It is not a decision made by a human being. John 1:13 tells us that it does not happen because of the "will of the flesh, or the will of man, but of God."

Being born again is a God-initiated contact that a human being finally responds to. Because we respond, does that make us the author? I hardly think so. We are born because of God's efforts, not because of our response. Does our "sensitivity to the Spirit's call" somehow make us more worthy? Again, I hardly think so. We are still basically selfish human flesh unless or until we allow the Spirit's work to change us.

That is why John 1:12 says that He gives the "right" or the "power" to "become children of God." To the degree that we submit and surrender to Him, His power can and will work in us. The fact that we have noticed God wooing our heart does nothing for us. Beginning to cooperate with Him does much in us. It is not that we have something good that He sees and uses. It is that we offer ourselves freely to Him to change and use us.

He must make us His children. And He does that with our complete and willing cooperation. We have the right "to become" fully His. We have the right "to become" fully like Christ. Many look more like selfish flesh. Many choose not to drink of His Spirit fully. The preferred choice is "I will do it by myself." The end result is that nothing of any substance happens.

Moses did not "suddenly" become a godly man. He was broken and molded and nurtured over his 120 years. God took Moses and put him together, piece by piece. For Moses, some of the key pieces were supernatural visitations. These brought power. These visitations from God changed him from a desert shepherd to a leader of Israel. So it still is today.

I am amazed that even Jesus did no recorded miracles until after the supernatural visitation of the Holy Spirit in the Jordan River. The dramatic miracles came after a dramatic visitation of the Spirit.

Yet the supernatural is not always "dramatic" but often consists of a more quiet spiritual communion. Even earlier, at the age of twelve in the temple, Jesus gave evidence of having had this quiet communion with God. He amazed even the learned elders with His knowledge. Did that knowledge come only from Mary or some other human teacher? I believe the Spirit's leading is part of the answer.

As soon as a person is being born again, we should begin to acquaint him with the Spirit's moving in his life. There should be a supernatural peace as a result of asking God's forgiveness. This peace is not just a natural result of confession. It is a supernatural response of God's Spirit in the heart of the new believer. This is a starting place for acquainting the new believer with the supernatural.

We also need to acquaint each new believer with the flow of worship toward God that should be coming out of the inner being of the new believer. Again, the new believer might not even notice what is happening or may even try to take credit for the good feelings that are coming out of him. Those "good feelings" are a thankful response to what has been done on the inside of the new believer.

If nurtured, "good feelings" progress into worship. God's Spirit is trying to teach the new believer to worship Him. If there is no recognition of the supernatural, the believer may take credit for having done something "good" and begin to think he "deserves" the result. Instead of worship, the new believer turns back to self and greatly limits the work of God in him.

We should also show the new believer that the Spirit of God will begin to illuminate his mind about the meaning of His Word (1 John 2:27). Moses was rewarded by God with more of Himself, simply because he turned aside to see a bush that did not burn. How much more will a believer be rewarded if he begins to acknowledge the subtle workings of the Spirit of God in his life? The more the new believer learns to focus on the spiritual, the more likely the spiritual will be released in him.

Despisers or Seekers?

We need the mountaintops. While we cannot create these experiences, we can do much to prepare our hearts for His coming in a greater way. We must first recognize what He is already doing and give Him thanks for His work in our lives. Then we need to "ask and keep on asking" for the fullness of the Holy Spirit (Luke 11:9-13). James tells us that "you do not have because you do not ask" (Jas. 4:2b). Many have never had deeper experiences in God because they have never asked for them.

Some are even in a class of not wanting any kind of extraordinary experience of God. In fact, at Mount Sinai, an entire nation told God that they did not want the supernatural display of His presence (Ex. 20:19). They preferred for Moses to go to God as their representative and bring God back in a safe and comfortable form.

Even so, many today want no part of anything that pushes them beyond the safe and comfortable norm. The Bible tells us to "earnestly desire the best gifts" (1 Cor. 12:31a). This passage refers to "spirit-breathed" gifts of chapter twelve. It has just spoken of healings and tongues and of interpretation of tongues. When it says "earnestly desire the best gifts," it is not talking about a "safe" experience of God.

With the coming of the Holy Spirit in Acts 2, Peter quotes the book of Joel, saying:

> 'And it shall come to pass in the last days, says God, that I will pour out of My Spirit on all flesh; your sons and your daughters shall prophesy, your young men shall see visions, your old men shall dream dreams' (Acts 2:17).

These verses do not speak of a "tame" Christianity. Added to the visions, dreams, and prophecies of this verse is "…wonders in heaven above and signs in the earth beneath: blood and fire and vapor of smoke" in Acts 2:19.

The New Testament is filled with examples of experiences that would push the modern American Christian beyond the comfort level. How would we respond today to Paul's experience of a blinding light and a voice from heaven? What would we do if an Ananias and Sapphira had dropped dead in a church? Or what would we do if we were struck dumb as Zacharias was or if we were in the house with the disciples when it began to shake during a prayer meeting?

God is the Almighty. To reduce Him to a human equation and to eliminate the miraculous is to deny a part of His character. Too many people have reduced Christianity to an intellectual set of Christian principles to be followed. God is a living and powerful God, and we still need to experience a little bit of that power first-hand! That kind of experience will change us. It certainly changed Paul.

What was revered and even sought after in the days of the early church is today sometimes referred to as "being of the devil." For many, anything supernatural is not of God. If that is true, how do you reconcile the obvious references to the supernatural that follow the coming of the Holy Spirit in the Acts 2 passage?

Many stay away from the supernatural out of fear of being deceived and receiving a counterfeit. Luke 11:11-13 says:

> If a son asks for bread from any father among you, will he give him a stone? Or if he asks for a fish, will he give him a serpent instead of a fish? Or if he asks for an egg, will he offer him a scorpion? If you then, being evil, know how to give good gifts to your children, how much more will your heavenly Father give the Holy Spirit to those who ask Him!

There certainly is a danger if a person is on some sort of ego trip and is willing to open up to whatever spirit or experience that comes along. However, if a person is truly relating to God, will God suddenly deceive him and send an evil spirit to give him a counterfeit supernatural experience? The Scriptures say otherwise! The key is to be seeking more of God from God. Danger comes only when some selfish end is being sought.

If the church has been doing its work properly, there should be no problem anyway. The love, joy, and peace (Galatians 5:22) that are the essence of the Holy Spirit cannot be confused with the manipulation and ego-stroking feel of the evil spirits. If the new believer has been introduced to the spiritual feel of the love and peace of the Holy Spirit's working, he will easily identify the difference between God's Spirit and the evil spirits.

The problem is that we have been told that the spiritual does not even exist. We have operated primarily from our minds and our emotions. The mind and the emotions cannot discern spiritual things. Our spirits can. If we have been exercising our spirits in real communion with God, there is no difficulty. If not, there will be complete confusion.

Actively Waiting to Receive

We are commanded to "earnestly desire the best gifts." It is not a passive attitude that says "whatever will be will be." It is an active laying hold of the things of God. It is an active seeking. It is an active humbling of self. It is an active surrender to more fully obey God.

We cannot actually "lay hold" of any spiritual gift or experience. It is a gift. It is given by Him. We can only prepare, watch, and wait with an open heart. He is God. He distributes as He chooses (1 Cor. 12:11). However, we can depend on being born again (Rom. 10:13) and on the in-filling of the Spirit of God (Acts 2:38-39), because He has promised those experiences to whoever asks. And God is always good for His promises.

Other experiences or "spiritual gifts" are not "guaranteed" for a specific believer. Isaiah's vision of heaven and Jacob's dream of the ladder to heaven were great experiences. Both were tremendously impacted, but even if we seek a similar experience, God is not obligated to answer that kind of request.

Accordingly, it is not good for us to set our hearts on a specific type of experience other than what God has promised to all. Instead, we should simply be open to the Spirit of God. He is

God.   He knows what each and every person needs.   He distributes of Himself according to the will of God.   In reality, it is more of God that we should be seeking, not some special type of experience.

Staying Open

If the extraordinary power of God has never been given a chance to do a work in us, it will do only a very limited work through us.   The mountaintops are vital.   They change us more into His image.   They give us direction.   They empower us.

At times, the mountaintop experiences can be a little scary. What did Peter think when Jesus was transfigured before him? How did the people respond on the day of Pentecost with all the supernatural signs attesting to the coming of the Holy Spirit upon the disciples?   Was it worth it to Daniel when a visitation from God left him so weak that he "fainted and was sick for days"? (Daniel 8:27a).

If we close ourselves to the supernatural, we largely close off the working of God.   After all, is not the voice of God supernatural? Is not the spiritual embrace of God that lets us know that we are true children of His a supernatural experience?

We shouldn't let it stop there!   We need to ask God to take us to His mountain, again and again.   Moses should be an example to us.   The tent of God's presence became His favorite abiding place.   What the people despised and rejected became the very spiritual life blood of Moses.   It made him the great leader that he was.

So it will be with each of us as we come to realize that this is meant to be the norm and not the exception. Do we fear some of the more unusual workings of the supernatural? Unfortunately, the answer is often "Yes!" Do we even deny the reality of God speaking to believers today? Practically speaking, we often do deny the voice of God simply because we have not been taught to listen spiritually.

Do you really want to go deeper in God? There is more available. There is a mountaintop waiting. Will you earnestly desire that kind of experience from Him? Don't set your heart on one particular experience. Set your heart on more of Christ. He waits on the mountaintop. His glory is there! He is calling to you to come and share in His glory.

Chapter Sixteen

The Valleys

"Do you think I have been any less present and active in your life this last summer than I was last spring?" It was one of those "thoughts" that jolted me and left me pondering if it was a "God thought" and exactly what it meant. As a church, we had experienced a phenomenal spring, bathed with the presence of God. During the summer and early fall, we had endured one trial after another. The mountaintop had quickly become a valley and I didn't like it.

We often refer to the times of glory and good feeling as the times when God is "present." We know that this is not true, because Jesus tells us in the closing verse of Matthew, "And lo, I am with you always, even to the end of the age" (Matt. 28:20b). God is everywhere, all the time, present. If our minds can handle it, He is somehow "more" present with the believer, promising to never leave nor forsake his own. He is not just present as an observer with those of us who are believers, but

He is "for us," constantly surrounding us with His love (Rom. 8:31-39).

There are times when we can feel the love of God and we are aware of the "truth" of His presence. There are times when we are not aware of His presence, and suddenly the "truth" of His presence seems like a lie. This is the place of growth for faith. As Jesus said to Thomas, "Blessed are those who have not seen and yet have believed" (John 20:29b). Blessed are we when we recognize the truth of His presence, even when we cannot feel it in any way.

Our faith and trust in God simply cannot be nurtured and grown if there is a constant and never-ending sense of the blessing of the Lord. Even behavioristic scientists have found this to be true in tests with animals. If a certain behavior is rewarded every time it happens, it is easier to eliminate that behavior than if it is rewarded periodically.

The classic example is the ringing of a bell as a signal that it is feeding time for a dog. Over a period of time, the dog associates the ringing of the bell with being fed. For a time, the dog will continue to come even if you only ring the bell. However, if you only occasionally ring the bell at feeding time, the dog will actually continue to come over and over again, with or without feeding. The behavior of coming at the sounding of the bell is actually more persistent for a longer period of time when the bell is rung intermittently.

God's goal is to build a tough, enduring faith in us. Though we may be offended at being compared to a simple animal being trained, the principle still works. If we are to be strong in faith, God simply cannot reward us with a constant flow of the awareness of His presence. It is not healthy for us spiritually.

Instead, He gives us exactly what we need at each and every moment. That is why we can say that His love never leaves us, though we may think that He has left us. Sometimes that means He withdraws the sense of His presence. Sometimes He allows us to be tested. Sometimes He disciplines us. After living on the mountain for a while, these experiences are often called "the valley." We don't like them, but they are just as much a manifestation of the love of God as the glorious times. They are perhaps the most important times of God's sowing into us to change and to renew us.

Faith, Discipline, Rock

> See that you do not refuse Him who speaks. For if they did not escape who refused Him who spoke on earth, much more shall we not escape if we turn away from Him who speaks from heaven, whose voice then shook the earth; but now He has promised, saying, 'Yet once more I shake not only the earth, but also heaven.'
>
> Now this, 'Yet once more,' indicates the removal of those things that are being shaken, as of things that are made, that the things which cannot be shaken may remain. Therefore, since we are receiving a kingdom which cannot be shaken, let us have grace, by which we may serve God acceptably with reverence and godly fear.
>
> For our God is a consuming fire (Hebrews 12:25-29).

Hebrews 12 could be called the discipline chapter of the Bible. Not surprisingly, it follows Hebrews 11, which is often called the "faith" chapter of the Bible. There is a relationship between the development of faith and the discipline of God.

As the chapter comes to a close, the writer of Hebrews quotes the book of Haggai to make the point that there is a time of "shaking" which will come. The writer says that there will be a "removal of those things that are being shaken, as of things that are made, that the things which cannot be shaken may remain" (Hebrews 12:27b).

The things that are "made" will be shaken. This body that clothes our inner man will be shaken. Anything in our inner man that is not rock solid will be shaken. Anything that is not of faith in THE ROCK will be shaken. If it can be shaken, it will be shaken.

You might ask, "How can a loving God treat us like that?" The answer is simple; a loving God knows that there is a time of judgment coming. And just as the first part of the chapter spoke of the discipline of the human father being for our good, so God knows that the time of "shaking" is for our good.

"For our God is a consuming fire" (v. 29). He may be loving, but He is also absolutely and completely just. What can be shaken, will be shaken. What can be burned, will be burned (1 Cor. 3:12-15). Only those things that are rock solid, with an eternal and weighty substance of the spirit will survive. Does that not remind you of Hebrews 11:1, "Now faith is the substance of things hoped for, the evidence of things not seen"?

Rock solid faith and discipline are absolutely intertwined. God is about the business of building a rock solid "stuff" in our inner man. Jesus even refers to Himself as the "chief cornerstone" (1

Pet. 2:6) and gives the disciple who was to become the leader of the twelve the name of "Peter" which means "little rock."

Faith in something seen is not really faith. If it can be seen, where is the exercise of faith? Faith becomes something of real substance, something with a rock-like quality that is a firm foundation stone, when it stands no matter what the circumstances look like.

This same imagery is very clear in 1 Peter 2:5-6:

> Coming to Him as to a living stone, rejected indeed by men, but chosen by God and precious, you also, as living stones, are being built up a spiritual house, a holy priesthood, to offer up spiritual sacrifices acceptable to God through Jesus Christ.

The faith that is being built within us is a solid thing that is building us and other believers into a "spiritual house."

Most houses can and will be shaken when an earthquake comes. The floods will destroy just about any house built. Fire will completely destroy other houses with a simple bolt of lightning. But the house that Jesus is building, using "living stones," will endure the shaking. Because it is built with stones of solid faith, no fire can destroy it. Because of its eternal strength, no flood can wash it away.

That is a picture of what God is doing in our inner man. He is building a creation with substance. That is a picture of what the father is attempting to establish in his child through discipline in the first part of Hebrews 12. He wants a child of substance. He wants a child that will not be shaken, blown around, and tossed about. He wants a child of faith.

Life Lessons

Thus the valleys. God is taking a simple piece of coal and turning it into a diamond. The heat and the pressure are necessary. The shaking begins and we begin to squirm.

Shaking takes on every form imaginable. Perhaps the best question is, "What do you care about the most?" Job said, "the thing I feared . . .." If you don't care about it, it really will not be a test. Can you imagine a father disciplining his child, saying, "That's it. No more broccoli! If you are going to behave that way, I'm taking away the broccoli."

Now there may be some of you who really like broccoli. But can you imagine seeing a child scream in agony saying, "No more broccoli? I just can't go on!" It hardly fits our experience. It is no punishment. It will have no effect.

Every person is different. Every person is unique. What is a test for one person is nothing to the next. What grows the faith of one person would absolutely destroy the next. Though we can certainly learn some things by watching others, many times if we compare life experiences with others it can actually confuse us or make us feel like we have been treated unfairly by God. Each person is dealt with individually in a manner that will grow his faith into something solid that cannot be shaken.

Faith in anything but God can and will be shaken. That is why the person with talent or possessions or status is more likely to struggle. "For you see your calling, brethren, that not many wise according to the flesh, not many mighty, not many noble, are called" (1 Cor. 1:26). When you have something that you can see that has substance, it is hard to put your faith in something that is invisible.

If, on the other hand, you are poor and miserable and blind, it is not particularly difficult to let go of what you do have in order to receive something that is, at best, "a hope." But that is what God calls us to do. He commands us to let go of all that we are trusting in and to take hold of Him and Him only.

Even those that would seem to have little to hang on to often struggle. "A bird in the hand is worth two in the bush." It seems much better to hang on to the few ashes that we do have, at least until the new inheritance is absolutely and completely secure. Unfortunately, God does not work that way. Until we let go, He does not release the new inheritance.

In many cases, we literally must be reduced to ashes before we will even begin to think about letting go. The cancer patient will try absolutely every treatment possible before succumbing and saying, "I guess it is in the hands of the Lord now." The patient has usually endured months of agony and anxiety by that time. His life has been a miserable wreck of grabbing on to one hope after another, only to see it wisp away. What can be shaken will be shaken.

Often, at the very least the emotional and spiritual agony need not have happened. Why not start from the beginning with, "Lord, it's in your hands now"? The answer is simple. We really do trust more in medicine and doctors than we do in God. We trust in good sense and health remedies. We even will try every kind of quackery because it is something we can "do" to help us feel in control. We will trust in anything that still leaves us somewhat in control of the situation.

God says, "I will be God." For Him to be God means that He is in control. That is an eternal truth that cannot be shaken. We prefer to live a lie that says that we are in control. Soon, the test comes, not to destroy us, but to reveal to us exactly where our faith is and where it needs to be.

The agony is "necessary" because our faith is tied to things that really do not support. Just as you only have so much energy in a day, and you can use it as you wish; in the same way, you only have so much faith in a day, and you can use it where you wish.

If your faith is being used toward doctors and medicine, it is not available to interact with God. Faith in futile things must be reduced to ash in order to open the possibility of faith in God. The discipline does not establish the faith in God, it simply makes it so that there is some "faith capacity" freed up that **could be** turned toward God.

This is not to be interpreted that going to doctors is wrong or for those weak in faith. In fact, a person who has had a bad experience with a doctor may find just the opposite. If God should so direct, it may take every ounce of faith the person has to be obedient to God and go to the doctor. It is not whether or not a person goes to the doctor that reveals faith, but it is whether or not the person is primarily relating to and trusting in God that makes the difference.

When a person does finally turn toward God, there is a spiritual deposit that takes place. Something of substance is established in the person. There is a connection made between the person and God in such a way that the inner man of the person is significantly changed. The fire can now come. The shaking can now begin. The wind can blow, but the fruit will remain. Something has been established that cannot be shaken.

To go back to the language of an earlier chapter, this is a good seed planted in good soil. The seeds of God are always good seed, but they are not always planted in good soil. When all ties to self and to the things of this world have been cut off, the seed does land in good soil. The ground has been plowed. It has been harrowed to smooth it back down. The inner man is ready to receive the seed and to produce a good crop.

Freeing Up Our Faith

The valley is not a place of great joy. Rather, it is a place of preparation of the heart. Too often, the heart has multiple attachments. Each of these ties becomes a hindrance to those who really do want to go deeper in God. The first commandment clearly tells us that we can have "no other gods before Him" or even competing with Him, for that matter. He is to be in a class all by Himself.

The one who wants to go deeper in God must free Himself up from all other attachments. No one can do that on his own. Only the shakings and the burnings and the floods will reduce our foreign dependencies, our foreign gods, to nothing. The valley really is our friend; at least if we want to go deeper in God it is. David says, in Psalms 84:6-7,

> Blessed is the man whose strength is in You, whose heart is set on pilgrimage. As they pass through the Valley of Baca, they make it a spring; the rain also covers it with pools. They go from strength to strength; each one appears before God in Zion.

The man who sets his heart on "pilgrimage," who has determined that God will be his strength, is sure to pass through the desert. The Valley of Baca was a notorious stretch of desert that left many dead and dying for lack of water. However, for the one that stopped long enough in the desert to dig a well, spring waters would flow up, more than enough to replenish the need for the journey.

How true a picture this is of life. The one that sets his face to grow deeper in God will often be immediately led into the desert. Jesus was. Right after His incredible baptism in the Jordan, with the heavens opening and the Spirit descending, He was led (some translations say driven) into the wilderness by the Spirit. It is no coincidence. He was digging His own well, a well of the Spirit within. The flow was more than enough for His journey. The abundance became apparent as soon as He was around people again.

We are led into the desert to lighten our load. We must be rid of all the extra baggage. We would try to carry too many earthly things along on our heavenly journey. God says that He is enough.

Most fight the desert. They try to hurry on through. The heat and the thirst only get worse that way. The only good way to experience the desert is to "make it a spring." We should stop. Take our time. Dig a well. If the Spirit really is trying to lighten our load, we should cooperate fully.

Often, when a believer is confronted by the Holy Spirit in a given area, he will try to confess it too quickly and to "get on with life in Christ." In some cases, what is being highlighted by the Holy Spirit is not even to the sin level. It is a tempting thought that stays in the mind a little too long or an action that is beginning to be visualized but is still kept under wraps. If the believer tries to confess "sin" at this stage, the confession is likely to be shallow with a weak "if I have sinned" mentality.

Perhaps it is not even sin that is being confronted. It may just be an emotional attachment that is taking up some of the space that Christ really should be occupying. Again, the confession of these kinds of things is likely to lack depth of ownership or understanding of their true significance. Having time in the desert with the Holy Spirit can be the only way that the believer begins to own and understand these areas for what they are, a true blockage of the flow of the Lord.

As the Spirit leads us into a desert time, the normal reaction is to scramble quickly to "get things set right." We are in a hurry to confess or to do something of consequence and the fact that it lacks real depth is not an issue with us. We forget that the Spirit has an eternal perspective and is not in the same kind of hurry that we are. He prefers depth. He desires a thorough work.

We are so in love with the "mountaintop" feeling that we hurry to get it back. Unfortunately, instead of being a real hunger for God, the race to return to the "mountaintop" often is more motivated by selfishness. Our inner man is not willing to endure "the sufferings of Christ" but prefers the "riches of good feelings."

The better reaction is to soak in the work of the Spirit. If the Spirit has us in a "mountaintop" season, it is because we need His love and a sense of His fellowship. During that time, we need to soak in every ounce of the fellowship of the Spirit that we can. We need to enjoy and to rejoice in and to savor the goodness of God. It needs to soak deep down into our person so that we become like the very joy of God Himself. Before long, the soaking results in our own person being so filled with joy that we exude the very life of God from our person.

The same is true of the desert. If the Spirit has led us into the desert, it is time to soak. The desert seems to be a dry and forsaken place, where there is no activity of the Spirit. The normal reaction is to move as quickly as possible to get out of the spiritual desert season. Often, believers in a dry season will do just about anything, even compromising standards to try to get back to the feel of the mountaintop.

The Spirit has a purpose for the desert. It seems to be a place that is nothing but a hot and miserable torment. But the Spirit commands us to stop and to dig. And while the digging is going on, we get even hotter and even thirstier. The better reaction would seem to be to move on and to get out of the desert as quickly as possible. The desert is a worse place for those who are digging, than for those who simply keep moving. But if that is where the Spirit has us, we need to soak in the experience of the desert.

And what does it mean to dig? Digging would seem to imply that we get busy doing "spiritual" activities. But the real spiritual digging begins when we come to the end of our own strength. Only then do we begin to depend more completely upon God. We begin to sense our own futility and our own helplessness. These are two things that the inner man absolutely hates. The heart of man will do almost anything to bring those feelings to an end. The wise man will stop and soak. A sense of our own futility and of our own helplessness apart from God is called humility. The wise man soaks it in. The fool runs on through the desert.

With humility comes the blessing and favor of the Lord. With a stop in the desert comes a spring. This man goes from "strength to strength." Why? Because he is no longer depending on his own strength. He has taken time to soak during the desert season. He has taken time to say "No" to his selfish desire to get out of the desert quickly. A "good-feeling" experience is not his god. Responding to the Spirit is his priority.

Preventing Panic

The desert is a time of seeing little or no fruit. Those who do not anticipate or understand this will panic. During the mountaintop season, the believer seems to have the Midas touch. Everything seems to result in something good. During the desert time, the believer suddenly develops a reverse Midas touch. Everything he touches seems to fall apart.

The eye that is set upon results will begin to panic. It will think that it is losing ground spiritually. It may even crash into a depression spiral. The eye that is set upon the Spirit will get the gentle reassurance it needs. When everything seems to be going wrong, the Spirit will gently say "Trust me." It is here that real faith begins.

Faith during the mountaintop is good. But faith that is seen and felt is at best a weak faith. Faith during the desert is a faith of substance. It is a faith with deep roots, so deep that even the scorching hot sun and the blistering winds will not bring disaster. Why? The roots have found the source. They have grown down deep to find the spring. No plant is afraid of the heat when it is tapped into the water source. Let the greenhouse begin. Make it hot! The growth will just flourish.

That's how it is in the desert. When everything wrong seems to be happening, if the roots go down to the Source, life changes. This is a plant that will not fail. This is a diamond that will not burn. This is a house built on the rock that will not be destroyed. This is joy and peace amidst the trial. This is a trial that is no longer a trial because the spring has been found.

Stephen was like that. He was being stoned. Stones hurt. He was leaving his family and friends. The church might even be hindered. And yet he was transformed into a perfect image of love and intercession. Seeing Jesus in the throne room with the Father, Stephen responded with almost the same words Jesus had spoken at His death: "Lord, do not charge them with this sin" (Acts 7:60b). And then he died.

This is the valley of the shadow of death. Sometimes it is a real death that we face, but more often it is a death to self. Some of the deepest works of the Spirit are found in the valley, but few have the courage to remain there long enough to really soak in all that the Spirit has for them. I return to the question at the opening of the chapter: "Do you think that I have been any less present and active in your life this last summer than I was last spring?"

The flesh says, "God, you left me this summer." The Spirit says, "I hovered more than ever." In fact, He not only was there, but during some of the desert times He carried us.

Do you really want to grow deeper in God? Recognize the full and complete work of God. Remember that He never does leave nor forsake you. Repeat to self statements of His love and faithfulness. Rest in His present work. If it is painful, endure. If it is joyful, celebrate.

In all things grow a taproot. Dig a well. Slow down until you see the current work of the Spirit and then cooperate with it. If it is discipline, humility, or rejoicing, embrace it. From the embrace comes real life!

Chapter 17

Today

Many make the mistake of evaluating their spiritual lives according to the mountaintop experiences. Others focus entirely upon mistakes and failures. Without question, both the mountaintops and the valleys have an influence on our lives that is much greater than the relatively small amounts of time spent in those experiences. Especially trauma points can devastate and dominate everything else that a person will experience.

Yet, in most cases, it is neither the mountaintops nor the valleys that are the most influential in the life of the person. It is today, tomorrow, and the next day. It is my job, my family, and my activities. Life is seldom lived in the extreme, but in most cases the greatest part of life is very normal and mundane. In fact, the ones that do live life constantly in the extreme, whether high or low, are more likely to be neurotic than to be a spiritual rock.

Walking into the Depths

> With what shall I come before the LORD, and
> bow myself before the High God? Shall I come
> before Him with burnt offerings, with calves a
> year old?
>
> Will the LORD be pleased with thousands of
> rams, ten thousand rivers of oil? Shall I give my
> firstborn for my transgression, the fruit of my
> body for the sin of my soul?
>
> He has shown you, O man, what is good; and
> what does the LORD require of you but to do
> justly, to love mercy, and to walk humbly with
> your God? (Micah 6:6-8).

The main question of the passage is very simple: What does it take to please God? The answer is also simple. Do justly, love mercy, and walk humbly with your God.

The choice of the word "walk" to describe our life with God is a good description of the day-to-day, mundane nature of much of our life. In the epistles alone, the word "walk" is used forty-four times to describe a person's general manner of living. Over and over, we are commanded to "walk" in a manner that is worthy of being called a child of God.

Seldom are we commanded to run. Seldom are we commanded to rest. Frequently are we told to walk. Today, an ordinary day, may be the most important day of your life, not because of its impact on your life, but because of the pattern that it follows.

Habits are, without question, the single most powerful force in any person's life. Even in the life of the neurotic person, who constantly lives life on the edge, there are habits that cause the person to continue in that manner. Even in the person with seemingly no pattern, there are patterns that allow for the radical swings.

The person who tries to live on the mountaintop will never be of any significant spiritual substance. That person's substance will be that of a "want to be." He will always be looking to cash in on "the big one," much the way a gambler wastes away his financial substance hoping to cash in on "the big one." That person will miss, yes, even squander the spiritual substance that is today. Instead of laying up a deposit toward heaven and creating a foundation to build on, that person is in the process of destroying what little he does have.

In the same way, some are stuck in the valley perhaps thinking that they are in a mode of repentance. The discipline process, at some time, has produced real fruit in their lives, and they long to see that kind of growth once again. Just as some are hypochondriacs and visualize constant physical sickness, others glory in spiritual trial and will literally behave in such a way as to create a trial if need be. Through resolution of the supposed crisis, there is a sense of accomplishment and meaning.

The problem is that a human induced crisis produces all kinds of negative fallout. And a lifestyle of constant trauma hardly produces a character of godly substance. While it is important to embrace the desert seasons of the Spirit of God, it is also important not to induce trauma seasons of your own.

Today really is the most important day of the rest of your life. It may seem inconsequential when compared to the whole, but those kinds of days really are the most significant part of any believer's life. And they are definitely important to the one who wants to grow deeper in the Lord.

Keeping the Love Fires Burning

Deuteronomy 6 is famous because of the quote that Jesus spoke from it, but the verses that follow may be just as important to understand Jesus' quote:

> You shall love the LORD your God with all your heart, with all your soul, and with all your strength.   And these words which I command you today shall be in your heart. You shall teach them diligently to your children, and shall talk of them when you sit in your house, when you walk by the way, when you lie down, and when you rise up. You shall bind them as a sign on your hand, and they shall be as frontlets between your eyes.   You shall write them on the doorposts of your house and on your gates (Deut.6:5-9).

We embrace the first words of this passage about loving God. We need to study the next few verses about **how** we are to love God. First, the words of God are to be in our hearts. They are not to be some rote or mundane thing to us. That can be one of the most difficult things to do. It is easy to let the Word of God become a common thing that we do as a matter of habit (though this is certainly preferable to not having the Word of God integrated into your life at all!).

In a marriage, one of the greatest dangers is to become unappreciative of the wife of your youth and to let the romantic fires die down to nothing. The "normal" day can become common place and routine. Before long, the wife or husband no longer seems to be a gift worthy of appreciation. God does not intend for a marriage to be passionless, nor are we to be passionless toward Him or His Word.

The fires of a marriage are kept alive through a constant voicing of appreciation and through continuing acts of sacrifice. Most of us have it backwards. We think that if someone treats us well, we will love them. That is not how we function. Matthew 6:19-21 tells us:

> Do not lay up for yourselves treasures on earth, where moth and rust destroy and where thieves break in and steal; but lay up for yourselves treasures in heaven, where neither moth nor rust destroys and where thieves do not break in and steal. For where your treasure is, there your heart will be also.

The Scriptures teach us to "lay up . . . treasures in heaven." Why? Because it is what we give that determines how we feel toward something, not what we get. If we have invested in something, if we have laid up a "treasure," we will begin to develop an emotional attachment. Our feelings actually follow our actions. If our actions are sacrificing with a willing heart, a love is bound to follow.

Certainly as human beings we react to situations instantaneously. We have feelings that seem to just "happen" and that do not seem to be a result of our actions. There are natural attractions and natural repulsions. Yet the deep, abiding things of the heart are not determined by those first reactions, but by our responses that follow those first reactions. Puppy love is a love that is not followed up by a response. In its own way, it is very real, but it is merely an attraction. It has no depth in the heart. It has no spiritual substance.

God calls us to have His Word in our "hearts". Many see that verse and immediately try to find the keys to keeping some kind of emotional passion burning. The end result of trying to keep a fervent emotional fire burning will be burnout. The passion is maintained through right actions with a right heart attitude, not with a constant stirring of emotion.

Similarly, the marriage that sets emotional passion as a goal will likely slide into sexual perversions within marriage and eventually into infidelity. Why? If passion is the goal, doing perverted and ungodly things in order to feel passion is easy to justify. In contrast, if giving love is the target, the act of selfless giving to the other will produce the very passion that eludes the couple that targets passion at any cost.

In the same way, the key to keeping the emotional fires burning toward God is actually found in the next few verses of Deuteronomy: "You shall teach them diligently to your children." The word diligent means to work at it. It is not a word that talks about doing something when a passion is stirred. It means to do it consistently, regardless. It is a sacrifice and an investment on a constant basis. Diligence requires concentration and single-mindeness of effort. Once again the idea of being able to focus surfaces as a part of spirituality!

Diligence does not require a passionate zeal, but rather a more steady plodding. Look at the next few verses. Diligence is to "talk of them when you sit in your house, when you walk by the way, when you lie down, and when you rise up." To be diligent is to be frequent and constant. It is as normal as eating and sleeping. It is purposing to plod away, day after day.

That hardly sounds like a life of great love for God. In fact, it sounds rather dull and lackluster, and it certainly can be. Jesus chastised the Ephesian church in Revelation for doing the works they ought to be doing but having left their "first love" (Rev. 2:4). It is certainly possible to plod along with God in a boring way. Many marriages are like that as well. Duty has taken the place of real love.

Dumping the Duty Mindset

However, that is not what God is calling for here. Duty is action without heart fervency behind it. It is a divided focus. "I will do the things I need to do for you because you are my wife or husband. I made my choice and I will stand by it." This is the mindset, but the mind really is on fishing or hunting or shopping or a vacation. It is a divided focus and as James says, "let not that man suppose that he will receive anything from the Lord" (Jas. 1:7).

It is possible to do things we do not like to do or want to do with a willing heart. Many times God asks us to do things that do not appeal to us. If we weigh the choice as being proper and worthwhile, our heart attitude will remain positive.

An example of this is found in dieting. To lose weight or to eat healthier, a sacrifice must be made. The mouth and the stomach cannot be given first priority. The person that is successful focusing on the benefits of the diet will be able to continue with a good attitude. The one that sees only the sacrifice may continue for a time, but at best, it will be with a "duty" attitude.

In the same way, if we declare a particular sacrifice as being "worth it" or think of it as an "investment" (Matt. 6:19-21), it no longer is an action of duty. Pictures displaying incredible weight loss motivate us because they focus us on the worthwhile goal. Being able to visualize a happy and harmonious home life can motivate a husband or wife to make the needed sacrifices within marriage with a cheerful heart, and not out of duty. When our spouse is declared to be worth the sacrifice in the depths of our heart, the result will be a heart full of a deep and abiding love. When God is declared worth any sacrifice, that too brings the ultimate life into our hearts.

Fanatic? Or Just Full of Love for Him?

God has said that if we really love Him, we will eat, sleep, drink, and think God all the time. We are to "bind" the statutes of God as a "sign" on our hand, between our eyes, on our doorposts and on our gates. The average person today would say, "Isn't that a little much? Aren't you taking things a little too far?"

In fact, the dreaded description of "fanatic" will likely surface.

Why?   Certainly the most prominent reason is conviction. People don't want to see someone else modeling a standard that they are not living up to. Others will criticize because they have tried to step into that level of walking with God and have done so out of duty. They will judge you to be making an unwise sacrifice. Some will respond with disdain because they have seen the crash of the "mountaintop fanatics" that maintain an intense walk but only for a short time.

Can it be that to walk with God the way He desires we must be a "fanatic"? In "commitment zeal" the answer would be "Yes." We must be committed to Him even to the point that our love for our close relatives is as nothing comparatively (Matt. 10:37). That certainly sounds like a fanatic! But the dictionary definition of fanatic is "irrational zeal." So I ask a question: Does God require any sacrifice of us without promising an appropriate reward? The answer is "No." A thousand times "No."

Everything that God asks of us is more than amply rewarded. Any sacrifice for Him is absolutely worth it. Even so, many would say, "I have made great sacrifices for God. And look! I have nothing to show for it!" Why can they say that and feel justified? Because they have made sacrifices out of a double-mindedness which God has told us clearly that He cannot reward. And the person who gets no reward certainly feels that the sacrifice is "fanatical."

Others have seen the Word of God, and tried to perform up to the required level more as a worship of self and its ability to perform good works. There is a sense of false duty to live up to a standard, mainly because to fall below the standard would hurt the ego. This is a sacrifice to self and not to God. It is a desire to live up to a standard in order to obtain praise. Again, there will not be a reward that seems appropriate for the sacrifice, because God would have to reward selfishness. Again, there will be a person that defines this level of sacrifice as "fanatical."

A person who walks before God in order to achieve a level of goodness can be a "fanatic." A person who declares God's command a worthwhile sacrifice and does it with a willing heart can never be called a "fanatic." The rewards are too great. The sacrifice is totally reasonable.

As an example, the husband who honors his wife continually will reap the reward of his investment. The relationship will flourish. He will declare the sacrifice worthwhile and reasonable. A deep and abiding love will grow between husband and wife that is its own reward.

In contrast, the husband that caters to his wife because of fear of reproach may appear to be investing in his wife. In actuality, he is more concerned about self and will reap little or no reward from his investment because it really is an investment in self.

God has shown us how to love Him. We are to speak of Him continually. We are to study Him constantly. We are to guard our hearts from any attitudes that would somehow reflect that the sacrifice is not worth it. And the fruit of these actions will be a heart that is overflowing with love toward God and man. Again, this sacrifice will be declared worthwhile and reasonable because of the experience of the love of God.

We are not to cower before Him in fear. We are not to respond merely for rewards or because of fear of punishment. Like the cowering husband, this is not an investment in God but an investment in self. No selfish, fear-based service can ever satisfy the command of God to love Him fully, nor will the person living in this way feel like the sacrifice has been reasonable. Indeed, a good judge of how we are living may be the way we feel about the sacrifices we are making for God. The one who feels a resentment about the sacrifice God is asking for needs to re-evaluate the motive of his service.

I know of very few people today who are walking out anything close to the Biblical mandate of Deuteronomy 6. We simply do not include the things of God in our lives to that degree. Yet that is the description of the number one commandment: "You shall love the Lord your God with all your heart, with all your soul, and with all your strength." We declare it to be unattainable. We declare it to be the life of the "minister." We declare it to be overly "fanatical." Mostly we excuse ourselves from really needing to love God the way He asks us to.

It is time that we begin to wake up and realize that this is the standard for the "normal" Christian. We also need to realize that it may take a period of years before we can approach that standard. Today is the first day. Tomorrow is the next. Old habits must be overcome one at a time. New habits must begin one at a time. How are you spending today?

Today may be the most important day of your life. Not last Sunday. Or the day you were saved. Today. Today is the day that you are forming patterns for tomorrow and for the next day. Those patterns either conform to the love of God or they do not. They either are growing you closer to God or they are taking you farther away. Today, average day, is your "walk" with God. It is not running or resting time, it is walking time. Where is your walk taking you? When it is all said and done, your average day may be the most accurate description of your spiritual life!

Chapter 18

The Role of the Disciplines

Since the invention of the printing press, a kind of cerebral Christianity has developed, especially in the Western world. Yet, it is important for us to remember that Christianity survived for almost 1500 years among a people who often had little more of the Scriptures than they could carry around in their heads. If we could accurately compare, I'm sure many of those who had little or no Scriptures would put much of our modern world to shame in spiritual maturity.

The spiritual disciplines are not just an exercise of the mind. In some circles today, you almost get that impression. The believers who lived under the oppression of the Iron Curtain provide a good modern example. Their fasting and prayer lives and their willingness to sacrifice for the Name of Christ, illustrate a spiritual maturity that many of the most learned believers in other parts of the world would love to imitate.

Yet, those behind the Iron Curtain also illustrate the need for the intellectual teaching. Without having direct access to the Word of God for ongoing study, historical traditions are likely to dominate. Combine that with family traditions and it becomes a mix that greatly hinders the church's progress. Truth must be intellectually known **and** actually lived to be effective for Christ.

Developing a Spiritual Day

If the best approximation of our spiritual lives is an average day, we need to pay special attention to our daily routines, or our daily disciplines. Many times, we limit our "spiritual examination" to the success or failure in having a daily devotional time, and that is important. Yet, our devotional time is at best a small fraction of our day. So how can our average day become an exercise in spiritual growth?

I've seen people enter a time of prayer with a chip on their shoulder, go through an exercise they call prayer with the same chip, and leave their prayer time just the same spiritually as they entered. I've known others that were walking judges. Even though they were in church every time the doors were open, church was simply another opportunity to exercise a critical spirit. The sermon, a Sunday school class, or even the missionary were constantly put to the test and generally received a thumbs down rating.

These people illustrate doing religious activity without achieving spiritual growth. The ultimate test of spiritual growth is, "Do I look and act more like Jesus?" Some people have an ugly disposition despite the fact that they are very well versed in the Scriptures. An intellectual knowledge, if it is filled with arrogance, is actually a hindrance to true spiritual growth.

Perhaps nothing better explains our most needed daily discipline than the "What Would Jesus Do?" bracelets. To put it in the words of Paul in Ephesians, we need to put off the old man and put on Christ (Eph. 4:22-24). We need to look spiritually just like Christ looks. My sons are very much a reflection of my image. In the same way, we need to be a refection of the God that has adopted us.

Religious activity can blind us. The person who enters prayer with a worried and fearful spirit, continues in that mode, and leaves unchanged has merely done a religious exercise. True prayer should change us into the image of Christ. Worry should dissolve into trust. Ugliness should be transformed into Christ-likeness. The greatest discipline of all is to turn all of life into a transformation process. Life should be our constant mode of changing more into the image of Christ.

How does that happen? Certainly the spiritual disciplines of Bible study, prayer, and fasting will be some of our most effective tools. Yet the most basic change agent is the Holy Spirit and our awareness of Him. Brother Lawrence, in the 1600's, wrote an entire book and lived an entire life based upon the simple concept of practicing the presence of Christ.

A constant awareness that Christ is both with me and in me through His Spirit can be very sobering. Which of us would knowingly choose to be a worrier, or bitter, or hateful before the throne of God? Would we not expect judgment? And yet we do those things in the very presence of the Spirit of God daily. Practicing the presence of Christ brings a constant awareness of our need for holiness and of our incredible need for His help to achieve that holiness.

With this discipline in place, every single event that life throws our way becomes an opportunity to be changed more into the likeness of Christ. In every event of life, we can choose to act as Christ would, or we can choose to react in our own selfish, human way. Each event becomes an opportunity to write more of the life of Christ into our own person or to become more deeply entrenched in the way of selfishness.

"What Would Jesus Do?" It is the ultimate spiritual discipline. Stop and take a look in a mirror from time to time. While the spiritual realm is invisible, over a period of time arrogance can almost be seen written on the face; so can love, joy, and humility. A good look in the mirror may just be the beginning of a new dimension in your spiritual walk.

We need to begin to see the events of life as a kind of mirror, as a reflection of some of the "stuff" that is in our hearts. As covered in an earlier chapter, any one event is probably not an accurate reflection of the heart in total, but it is a reflection of the current time of abundance. It is a part of the heart, whether good or bad. When we see true humility surfacing, we need to rejoice! We can be assured that it is not the product of our own effort but of the work of God in us. If we see ugliness, we need to stop, confess, and be cleansed in that area. When we do, life will change us for the better instead of reinforcing a bad habit.

Again, the most important part of this discipline is the practicing of the presence of God. If we try to clean up our own life apart from the enabling of the Holy Spirit, it will only end up in further imprinting the image of spiritual arrogance into our person. If, on the other hand, we are in constant communion with the Holy Spirit, letting Him speak words of approval or rebuke to us, and then we responding accordingly, we will see a great change toward the image of Christ. Self-effort produces vanity. God-consciousness and God-dependence produces a godly fruit.

The Word as a Change Agent

With this as a backdrop, the other spiritual disciplines become of great value. The mind truly is one of the greatest hindrances or helps in the spiritual life. If the mind is not renewed (Rom. 12:2), you will never be able to become the spiritual person God has called you to be. The person who continues to dwell on areas of worry will never be able to reflect a positive faith in God. This person must begin to meditate and think on what God has said about His love and care for the believer. If the stronghold of worry is allowed to exist in the mind, the person will not be spiritually changed but will remain a fearful and worried person. The mind must be disciplined toward the Word of God.

This can be done through regular reading, study, memorization, and meditation on the Word of God. As Deuteronomy 6 points out, the normal Christian life should be one that is filled with these activities. It should not be isolated to just a few moments of devotion in the morning.

To continue meditating on the Word, a person must choose to change focus. A worrier can do a religious exercise of Bible reading, but a worrier cannot truly focus on the content of the Word of God and continue as a worrier. A change must take place or the habit of worrying is simply becoming more deeply entrenched.

The Word of God is to be a change agent. Reading and study are not to be a separate activity from, but a support activity for being transformed into the image of Christ. We need to recognize the Word is our mirror (James 1:23), but if it is not applied, we become like a man who "observes himself, goes away, and immediately forgets what kind of man he was. But he who looks into the perfect law of liberty and continues in it, and is not a forgetful hearer but a doer of the work, this one will be blessed in what he does" (James 1:24-25). The Word is to be obeyed first and foremost.

I would much rather see a person read merely one verse a day with understanding and application than to have him study great amounts to be used as a weapon against the shortcomings of others. Often, as people become "mature" in Christ, the Word of God becomes a tool to judge others who are "not like me" as being inferior. If those people could only stop at the mirror for a moment, it would be obvious what kind of image is developing and it is not an image of the love of Christ.

Each day should be a mixture of the presence of Christ and the written Word of God. I strongly recommend a regular daily habit of a devotion, done at the same time and in the same place each day. We are creatures of habit. The habit will help steer us back to the presence of God on our bad days. On our good days, it will only carry us even higher.

Some would say that they are constantly aware of God's presence, and that is enough. Which of us is really that pure? Without an intentional time with God as central focus, it is nearly impossible to maintain an awareness of Christ's presence over a period of years. The time apart is vital. Without the Word of God, we will deceive ourselves into thinking we are doing well when we are not. We need our spiritual mirror on a regular basis.

Prayer and Fasting as Support Tools

Regular time in prayer is vital.   While experiencing God's presence is a type of prayer, it is far from a total experience in prayer. Prayer recognizes God's presence and begins to talk to God as if He were right there, because He is. It is a sharing of thoughts, feelings, confessions, and needs to a God Who is present because His Word promises that He is present.

Yet, God clearly rebukes any who would think that their ability in prayer will achieve anything:

> And when you pray, do not use vain repetitions as the heathen do. For they think that they will be heard for their many words. Therefore do not be like them. For your Father knows the things you have need of before you ask Him (Matt. 6:7-8).

God wants to use our prayers both to change us and to change others into His likeness. "Vain repetitions" produce nothing but vanity in spirit. They are not the God-kind of prayer.

 If we are not careful, we think of ourselves as the change agents, doing a great work for God. Instead, we need to realize that any great work that will be done, will be done in God and through God.   As we wait upon His leading, and pray His prayers, great things will happen. When we set out to be the "faithful" man of the hour and to do a great work, little will happen.

That is not to be interpreted that prayer should not be regular or systematic. Many are led by God to pray around the world or through prayer lists in a systematic way. Without some organization, very little prayer life will exist. God is an orderly God. Our prayer lives should reflect that order.

A prayer habit is vital to keep us exposed to the Spirit of God in a way that we can and will respond to His leading in prayer. With no habit, prayer will probably not occur at all. With too structured a habit, there is no room for the Holy Spirit to speak, to lead, and to pray through you. Praying around the world systematically can give the Spirit the chance to lead us daily to pray His prayers for each of the countries. If structure becomes preeminent, this method can degenerate into a ritual of praying the same prayers daily, which will probably result in development of a sense of self-importance in the person. With self-importance, true prayer ceases.

Fasting also is very important. God has given us fasting to "loose the bonds of wickedness" and "to undo the heavy burdens" (Isaiah 58:6). Fasting can have a similar effect to the Word of God. The Word acts as a mirror. It makes our sinful part visible. Fasting acts as a furnace. It brings the dross to the surface. If we allow God to skim off the dross, we are truly "loosed from the bonds of wickedness." If not, fasting becomes just another religious exercise.

The goal of all the disciplines needs to be greater Christ-likeness in everything and in every way. Fasting can bring a release of spiritual power and we need spiritual power. Yet, fasting for that reason can easily degenerate into selfishness, which destroys the real reason God would have us fast. We need to know Him in a greater way. And true knowledge is to live just as He would live.

I have heard many say something like, "If I fully understand, then I will obey." That too is very dangerous thinking. How many fully understand the work of the cross before they accept Christ? How many get a much greater revelation of the work of Christ on the cross because of their obedience?

Most of the Scriptures really are simple to understand if we would only obey them. And obedience is the final test, the final discipline. I can expose myself to the love of Christ. I can memorize specific Scriptures about His love and still refuse to love my brother. My refusal prevents me from being like Christ. It prevents me from truly knowing Christ, at least in that area.

Needing God to be Godly

Unfortunately, all of us have areas. We all have a point that we "get off the train." God is using life to move us more into His image and we hit a point where the cost simply seems to be too great. The final step of obedience is just too much. We think about it, pray about it, even visualize it, but we simply cannot do it. We fail the test.

The humble man does not stop there. He recognizes that God does have the answer. Every command is a promise, a promise of God's enabling to walk in that command. God would not ask us to do anything that His Spirit cannot enable us to do. He does ask us to do many things that we in our own human limitations could not possibly achieve.

God will not share His glory. If we think we can obey apart from His help, He will let us try. He will let us just keep forgiving in our own human strength until a situation in life comes along that simply whips us. We can no longer forgive. Now we begin to display real truth: We cannot be godly without God.

Failure is not a disaster to the humble man. It is only a reminder that "I must have tried it in my own strength." With God's help, we truly cannot and will not fail. Obedience based on true dependence on God will be achieved. It is not impossible. I can truly "do all things through Christ who strengthens me" (Phil. 4:13).

The spiritual disciplines seem to be an exercise in human effort and they are. God wants and requires our full cooperation and our ultimate effort. The disciplines are absolutely vital to healthy spiritual growth, but that does not negate God's place of involvement. Actually, it enlarges it. By cooperating with God, we cleanse the vessel so that He can more freely pour through it. Over a period of time, our efforts become more image-of-God efforts, because we know our utter dependence on Him.

We should never, ever evaluate our lives according to the quality of an isolated habit of devotion to the Lord. If we do, God Himself may have to come and frustrate our disciplines in order to break down our developing spiritual pride. Yet, we should never make the opposite mistake either. Without the disciplines, without regular times of prayer, study, fasting, and memorization, we will not grow in God to the level that He has created us to achieve.

Going deeper in God is truly a life study, a life discipline. We need to begin our day in the laboratory of a time isolated with God and then expand His presence into the entire life experience. We have nothing to lose, but our own flesh!

Chapter 19

The Body

As Americans, we have cut our teeth, chewing on notions of rugged individualism. The American dream tells us that we can go anywhere we want to go, do anything we want to do, and say anything we want to say.

Spiritually, the Reformation has taught us about the individual priesthood of the believer and of our absolute freedom as an individual to be born again. The lesson seems loud and clear: "I don't need anybody else to serve God. I can do it by myself."

This message is repeated over and over again in different ways as people declare that they do not need involvement with a church (or the church) in order to serve God. The attitude is "I can believe what I want to believe. It's between me and God."

I chose the order of "me and God" for a reason. "I can do it by myself." "Me and God." The fact that the "me" comes before God should give us some insight into the level of spiritual maturity. As we grow, we come to realize that God has to come first. And as we grow even more, we come to realize that the "me" part continues to shrink and the God part continues to expand. The very language of "me" and "by myself" are dead giveaways.

Proverbs 18: 1 tells us, "A man who isolates himself seeks his own desire; he rages against all wise judgment." It would be nice if we could just go off in a corner of the world somewhere and grow up in Christ. Think of all the pain and heartache that we would miss! Unfortunately, the truth of the Scriptures is that to do so simply means that we will end up seeking our own desires. Instead of becoming more mature in Christ, we will likely become more full of self.

This is not meant to say that a believer does not need from time to time to take a sabbatical from the world and to get off by himself with Christ. The teaching of Matthew 6 is very clear that it is good and right to go to a "secret place" where no one else is and to spend time alone with God. This is a vital part of the believer's walk with God.

The important thing is that the isolation is for a season, and that it is with God and not a communing with self. Jesus often isolated Himself for prayer, but He would return to pour out the fruits of His isolation among humanity. Time alone with God is our strength. Indeed, the very purpose of many of the spiritual disciplines referred to in the last chapter is the enlarging of time alone with God.

Isolation from the body of Christ "rages against all wise judgment." Many believers get hurt in a church in some way and the rugged individualism that is so much a part of the American way takes over. They no longer need any involvement with the church or anyone else for that matter to serve God as they want to.

Key words: "As they want to." "Seeks his own desire." "Rages against all wise judgment." Full of self. No room for more of God.

Created for Impact, Not Isolation

The Scriptures very clearly teach that each person was created specifically for the very time that he or she is alive:

> Your eyes saw my substance, being yet unformed.
> And in Your book they all were written, the days
> fashioned for me, when as yet there were none of
> them (Psalm 139:16).

Before my substance was even formed, the days were "fashioned for me." This is similar to Jesus' statement that man was not made for the Sabbath, but that the Sabbath was made for man. Man is the center and crowning glory of His creation. We don't just happen to exist during a time and hope to make the best of it. We are specifically created in a certain time for a reason.

Ephesians 1:6 tells us that God "chose us in Him before the foundation of the world." Ephesians 2:10 says, "For we are His workmanship, created in Christ Jesus for good works, which God prepared beforehand that we should walk in them." God chooses the specific time and place in history when He desires us to live. We are perfectly matched with our generation with a specific set of talents that will positively impact our time. To ignore this fact and to live in isolation is to thumb our nose at God.

We are "created in Christ Jesus for good works, which God prepared beforehand that we should walk in them" (Eph. 2:10b).

Jeremiah was specifically created for his generation. Jeremiah certainly had reason to complain. He was a godly man with a soft heart amidst a perverse and disgusting generation. That combination led to a life of constant heartache and tears, which has caused him to be dubbed the "weeping prophet."

Yet think about the wisdom and love of God. He desperately desired to see the nation of Israel brought back to Himself. He knew that if He sent an Elijah type, the hard hearts would simply reject him and probably stone him on the spot. Even the more noble type of person, Isaiah, had been sawn in half (as history records) in a more genteel time than this.

If God wanted to reach His people with a message, how was He going to do it? The answer was with a weeping prophet. Even a hard-hearted people could not murder a soft-hearted weeping man. He was a nuisance to them. But to murder him? Thus Jeremiah was left alive. He was tortured and suffered greatly internally as well. But he was left alive to present the Word of God over and over again.

Judgment had to come and did. Yet God was absolutely just and loving because He had done everything He could to get the message across and to give the last few people a chance to repent. And the vehicle to deliver this message? Jeremiah.

Comparisons That Cause Complaint

If God has called you to be a Jeremiah, you certainly have room to complain, at least if your basis is to look around at others and compare. Peter tried to do that in the last chapter of John. Jesus had just told Peter that when "you are old, you will stretch out your hands, and another will gird you and carry you where you do not wish" (v. 18). Now that is something awful to look forward to! Peter thinks, "When I am old, I will be crucified!"

His immediate response is similar to what ours would be. "What about this man?" (v. 21). We are very quick to notice suffering that seems to be unfairly placed upon our shoulders. This is Peter's reaction. Jesus' response is rather pointed: "If I will that he [*John*] remain till I come, what is that to you? You follow me" (v. 22). In modern language, Jesus might say, "That's none of your business. Get your mind back where it belongs and follow me."

That seems harsh. If I had just been told I was going to be crucified, I might be a bit distracted. Yet Jesus gives Peter no space for self-pity. "You follow me." Peter was created for Peter's life. He was designed for it. It seems a hard thing. It seems unfair. But it **is** a perfect fit. Jeremiah's life seems hard. It seems unfair. But it too is a perfect fit.

From our own point of view, we would say that one person has it easy and another has it hard. Who knows how a Jeremiah would have reacted to a time of prosperity? Is it possible that he would have been enticed into a life of sin by a wife that was caught up in the ways of the day? It is not only possible but likely considering the type of person he was. It was the mercy of God to give him the social conditions He gave him. Today and forever in eternity, Jeremiah is reaping a great eternal reward because of the job God gave him to do.

In the same way, Peter was a rough and tough battler. He needed challenge and confrontation to be at his best. The threat of persecution only served to heighten his resolve to serve Christ. He blew it once at the crucifixion, but was ready at Pentecost. If need be, he would suffer for Christ. Take away the battle, and a Peter-type of person gets bored. It's Samson during the good times. The Delilah's get to him. So it is with Peter. Peter was created for the day, and the day was created for Peter.

So it is with every person alive. If Peter was not allowed to complain, and Jeremiah was shown no mercy, who are we to complain about the day and time in which we live? And which of us is given a ticket to claim the luxury of isolation from our generation? Are we not also created with a call to work with the body of Christ to do the work of God?

The Body

God has also clearly said over and over again that we are the body of Christ. The term "body" alone tells us much. Which cell can live in isolation from any other? We are created to live in an interdependent relationship with one another. We benefit others. Others benefit us. We harm others. Others harm us. We are very much a product and a part of our own generation.

Jeremiah suffered much because of the sins of his generation. As one living during that time, he cannot be separated from his generation. It is like there is an invisible rubber band that ties him to his time that will not let him get too far away. He can lead his generation toward God, but the invisible rubber band only allows him to go about so far.

As rugged individualists, we reject this truth. We do not like to see how dependent we actually are on others. We deny the truth and existence of "the body of Christ." We deny that we are created for and as a part of a day and time. We distance ourselves from our generation and want to think of ourselves as superior to our day and without the sins of the day.

Daniel did not do so. "O, Lord, to **us** belongs shame . . ." (Dan. 9:8). "**We** have not obeyed the Lord our God . . ." (Dan. 9:10). Daniel was a righteous man who shined among all the Bible characters. Yet, he absolutely included himself in the sins of his generation. He identified with his time and confessed and interceded just as if he had participated in the sins.

And in a way he had. We are the body of Christ. To separate us is impossible. To say that we have absolutely no participation in or with the sins of our brother is wrong. We are the body. We are created for this time. We are created to identify with this generation, to suffer its consequences, and to intercede before God according to the "works which God prepared beforehand that we should walk in them" (Eph. 2:10).

It is time we quit berating the body of Christ. To do so is to berate ourselves. It is to speak judgment upon our own selves. Ephesians 5:28 says, "So husbands ought to love their wives as their own bodies; he who loves his wife loves himself." The husband loves himself by loving his wife. If this is true for husbands and wives who are joined together in spirit through covenant, is it not also true for the body of Christ which is joined together in spirit through covenant?

The righteous men of the Bible, Moses, Daniel, and Job, are called upon to intercede for their own generations. And they are not called to do it from a distance, but from the inside. They do not confess the sins of "the people" but rather "our sins." Jesus could not even intercede from a distance. He had to come, take on the form of a man and be made like those that He was interceding for in every way. This is almost grotesquely clear in Second Corinthians 5:21:

> For He made Him who knew no sin to be sin for
> us, that we might become the righteousness of
> God in Him.

Jesus became sin for us! That almost sounds sick. It is too much for us. It seems that it must be untrue. But it is Scripture. He became sin, that we might become the righteousness of God in Christ.

Just as Christ did, we are to perfectly identify with our generation. We are not to separate ourselves from the generation but to identify with it. Going deeper in Christ demands not isolation, but identification.

Certainly, I am not saying that we are to join in the sins of the generation. Christ did not join in the sins of the generation. He identified with the generation and interceded for the sinfulness. The innocent one bore the sins of the guilty, that they might partake of his innocence. In the same way, we should live a "separated" life of holiness while participating in and identifying with our generation.

For us to truly be what God has called us to be, we must lay down our rugged individualism. Any person, by himself, will never measure up to what God has called him to be. We need other believers. We even need the unbelievers. We need our generation.

During World War II, it is no secret that much of the genius of the American success in weaponry technology actually came from those that had fled or been rejected by the German regime. Our victory actually depended greatly upon those whom we might have considered to be the enemy. We very easily could have shunned their input and history may have been greatly changed.

God has created us for this generation. There are those for whom He has a very important work that are still numbered among the unsaved. In fact, the very life and health of the body of Christ may be languishing for want of the giftings of a particular unsaved person. Think of the example of the Apostle Paul if you think that I am being foolish. Where would the body of Christ have been if he had not been saved?

We cannot afford to pronounce the judgments and to create the distance we have consistently created between the denominations and with our generation. We were created for today. We need to stop whining about our differences and the difficulty of our particular calling. We need to hear the voice of Christ saying what He said to Peter, "Follow me." Our generation hangs in the balance. If we don't learn to be the body of Christ and hang together, we will hang separately.

Putting it in Practice

In theory, that may sound reasonable. But it is not just a theory. There are very real and practical steps that must be followed if you are to grow in Christ to the level that He desires. The rubber band effect of the body is very real. We are bound together as if by an invisible rubber bundle. You will help grow others as you grow, pulling the whole bundle along. But if you try to grow out ahead of the pack, you will feel the restraining force of the rubber band.

In Acts chapter 2, fellowship is given as one of the basic ingredients of a healthy and growing church. Fellowship is a tool of growth or of disaster. Fellowship with godly men or women will impact your soul for God. Fellowship with darkness will surely lead you down a different path.

If that is true, how can we identify with a corrupt generation? The answer is simple: we walk according to the call of God, shining His light. If an unbeliever will hang around as we talk about the things of Christ and live out His ways, then spend the time! If we are called to be a shining light in the midst of darkness, then we must do so! We are the life of Christ manifested in this generation.

We identify with the generation by acting as an intercessor on behalf of the generation, not by fellowshipping with the generation. An intercessor stands between the generation and God. He has one hand on each and acts as a go-between. He is a part of two worlds at once for the purpose of mediation.

Fellowship is very different. It is to have in common. It is to absorb and to share. Ideally it is to be a communing of the light of Christ in me with the light of Christ in you. Your strengths should lift me and my strengths should lift you. Unfortunately, it also works the other way. Weaknesses impose the rubber band effect as well, unless of course, the grace of God prevails in a given situation. When it is God and His grace that are given priority, we all win, the flesh loses, and the body of Christ is greatly blessed.

Fellowship begins as an association with others. It is simply spending time together and giving one another our attention. Just as a key to meditation and individual growth is focus of attention, so fellowship demands a focus of attention upon the body of Christ and also those that Christ has called us to reach out to that are not yet a part of His body.

Hebrews 10:25 gives us the simplest level of fellowship telling us not to forsake "the assembling of ourselves together." In short, we need to show up together at the same place on a regular basis. In modern terms, we need to "go to church." We need to gather regularly with a group of believers. Not to do so is isolation. It is foolishness. It is selfishness.

Cliques or Closeness?

Yet, this is just the beginning. Jesus very clearly modeled having different levels of relationships with different sets of people. He had an inner core of three disciples: Peter, James, and John. This was not selfish but according to the natural constraints of time and also according to the will of God. No one can have hundreds of close friends. If anyone tries to do so, the relationships will, by necessity, be shallow. It takes time to have a close friend. Multiple close friends is an impossibility. Jesus especially reached out to three.

As in everything Jesus did, the three were chosen according to the will of God. Each of them would have a significant role in the kingdom after Jesus' return to heaven. They needed the extra time with Him.

Yet it is not all for practical reasons that these three were chosen. God is great enough to match the practical with the personal preference. I dare say that Jesus especially enjoyed these three among the twelve. John seems to indicate this as he refers to himself as "the disciple whom Jesus loved" several times in the book of John.

Jesus also had the twelve who had preferential time above and beyond all others. It was less intimate than the three, but more intimate than any of His other relationships. Other levels were the seventy, the one hundred twenty, the multitudes, and the world as a whole. Jesus clearly modeled different levels of fellowship as an example for us.

Paul had a Barnabus and a Timothy. He had a trainer, an encourager, and a trainee. This is our model for mentoring. We need a mentor. We need a disciple. We need peers. We need those who will challenge us to grow. We need to be an example to others and a challenge to them to grow. We need a place to rest and be ourselves.

Another way to say it is that we need a spiritual parent, a spiritual child, and a spiritual brother (or sister) or prayer partner. Mostly, we need openness and accountability. Just as growth in God is based on honestly facing the truth about ourselves with Him, we now need to enter a new level of openness and honesty. This time it is with other people.

This time it is much harder. It is one thing to trust God, but people? Do you want to grow in God? You have no choice. God has designed the body that way. Jesus modeled it. Paul followed suit. So must we.

The "A" Word

Accountability is a very important word if we are to grow in Christ. Without it, we will only become more pronounced in our weaknesses, and the strengths that we do have will become perverted. The person who is not accountable, inevitably will, for the sake of his own ego, overrate his strengths and set them over and against the strengths of the rest of the body. Is that a picture of the love of Christ or a perverted view of the importance of self?

We must see ourselves as inside the rubber band. At times we are pulling the group toward God and at times we are the ones being pulled. But we are all a part of the body and we cannot be separated. It is time we recognize this and begin to practice the deeper levels of fellowship that place us in accountability relationships. We must see ourselves as responsible to others for our walk!

Acknowledging Our Debt

Another similar truth is our need to recognize how much of our life in Christ really does come indirectly through other believers. We want to think that "me and God" (notice the order) have it all under control. Where would Joshua have been without Moses? What would Elisha have been like without Elijah? How would Timothy have turned out without Paul?

In each case, there is a very real impartation of the life of Christ through one person to another. Which of us does not owe our very born-again experience in Christ to another person? I know of few for whom Christ has made a personal appearance to invite them into the kingdom. Paul would be one, but not without the influence of Stephen, Ananias, Barnabus, and others. Indeed, we owe our very life in Christ to the body! How can we turn around and defame the very giver of life to us?

In some cases, that life is imparted to us through fellowship. It is "absorbed." We are spiritual beings and other spiritual beings impact us for the good as the light of Christ shines through them. In many cases, the life of Christ is directly imparted through prayer. We pray with people to be saved, healed, or to receive some special blessing from God. Our prayers are the means God uses to impart a blessing.

Many never achieve the kind of walk that God would have desired because they distance themselves from the body. We need the prayers and the fellowship of the body to achieve the deeper walk in God. We need "soak time" in fellowship. We need "soak time" in prayer with others. We need to humble ourselves to become accountable to others to help keep us on track in our personal disciplines as we walk with God.

There are Elijah's and Moses' and Job's that seem to stand almost completely away from the crowd. Yet even Elijah needed the widow at Zarapeth. Moses needed Aaron and Hur. And Job needed to pray for and return to fellowship with his three friends. Some are called to be anchors. Some tend to stand more alone than others, but none stands alone.

We must be individuals without embracing rugged individualism. We are the body. We will grow or regress together. For many this represents a radical change in thinking, but perhaps that is one of the reasons why the church today is so weak. Truth will bear fruit. As we join together, our depth in Him and our fruit will be greatly multiplied!

Chapter 20

Entering the Heart of God

Is it possible to pursue God, to walk in the disciplines, and even fellowship intimately with others and still miss God's best for our lives?

Again, "the heart is deceitful above all things" (Jer. 17:9a). We ascribe to ourselves perfect motives, but the heart is continually less than perfect. In coming to Christ, it is generally for very selfish reasons. We want heaven. We want to avoid hell. In continuing with Christ, it is again for selfish reasons. We want blessing. We want to avoid pain.

Our entire life can be caught up in a trail of seemingly perfect service to Christ, but just as Christ had to reprimand the church at Ephesus, we too may have left our "first love." Or even worse, we may have hardly even known "first love," but instead served Him primarily out of self love.

Jesus says, "for the Son of Man came to seek and to save that which was lost" (Luke 19:10). If we really intend to go deeper in Christ, we must enter not just into the works of Christ, but into the heart of Christ. The heart of Jesus was and is continually to "seek and to save that which was lost."

James says it this way, "Pure and undefiled religion before God and the Father is this: to visit orphans and widows in their trouble, and to keep oneself unspotted from the world" (James 1:27). Proverbs tells us that "He who has pity on the poor lends to the Lord" (Prov. 19:17a). In Matthew, Jesus says, "I was hungry and you gave Me food; I was thirsty and you gave Me drink; I was a stranger and you took Me in; I was naked and you clothed Me; I was sick and you visited Me; I was in prison and you came to Me" (Matthew 25:36-37). And when did the righteous do these things? When they did it unto "one of the least of these My brethren" (Matt. 25:40b).

Even in Jesus' own announcing of His purpose on earth He says, "He has sent Me to heal the brokenhearted, to proclaim liberty to the captives and recovery of sight to the blind, to set at liberty those who are oppressed; to proclaim the acceptable year of the Lord" (Luke 4:18b). Jesus' heart majors on bringing help to the helpless, on loving the unlovely.

Jesus' heart is not just interested in getting us to live a "righteous" lifestyle, full of the right kind of works. In the Sermon on the Mount He asks, "For if you love those who love you, what reward have you? Do not even the tax collectors do the same? And if you greet your brethren only, what do you do more than others? Do not even the tax collectors do so?" (Matt. 5:46-47). It is possible to have a seemingly righteous life among "the brethren" because they are so good at giving love back, and to totally miss the heart of God.

His love loved those whom He had no reason to love. "For scarcely for a righteous man will one die; yet perhaps for a good man someone would even dare to die. But God demonstrates His own love toward us, in that while we were still sinners, Christ died for us" (Romans 5:7-8).

In the midst of some parables, Jesus gives us this advice:

> When you give a dinner or a supper, do not ask your friends, your brothers, your relatives, nor rich neighbors, lest they also invite you back and you be repaid. But when you give a feast, invite the poor, the maimed the lame, the blind. And you will be blessed, because they cannot repay you; for you shall be repaid at the resurrection of the just (Luke 14:12-14).

Hopefully by now the message is becoming clear. It is very possible to live in the midst of a church "bless me" club, where everyone scratches the back of the other and all have seemingly righteous lifestyles and totally miss the heart of God. His heart is to love even those who hate Him, but He especially loves the hurting and the helpless wherever they may be found.

In Matthew 25, when Jesus says that if you have done a good thing (or evil) unto "these my brethren," I don't believe that He is talking about brethren in the sense of those that are Christians. I believe He is talking about His human brethren. If that is true, we are challenged not just to love those in the church, but to love all of humanity.

The greatest act of love that Jesus ever showed was laying aside the throne (Phil. 2:5-7) in order to take on human flesh. Can we even imagine leaving heaven to suffer for a bunch of misfits that hate us? "In all things He had to be made like His brethren"

(Hebrews 2:17a). Again, the word "brethren" is not talking about just the "believers."

All of humanity has become His "brethren." And it is His humanity that makes it possible for any human being to come to Christ. What human enemy is outside the potential for salvation? What person is not of human flesh and is not in a sense a "brother" to Christ? And which human being is excluded from the possibility of becoming a true "brother in the kingdom" if they will only respond? The target of Jesus' love was all of humanity, not just a select few "brethren" that would one day become a part of the church.

God's heart is for all of mankind. He desires for all to come to salvation (1 Tim. 2:4). His heart is to "seek and to save that which was lost" (Luke 19:10). His heart of love is like an endless appetite that knows no bounds. Having loved one into the kingdom, He sets His sights on another. He is not content with the praises of the perfected, but like a mother watching over her brood, He will not be satisfied until His love has gone out to all of His human brethren. They may not receive it. But it must go forth!

Understanding the Heartbeat

To enter into the heartbeat of Christ, we must be about the business of seeking that which is "lost." The whole concept of salvation has been popularized by our culture and has largely been turned into a single work of confession that is done to receive Christ. However, I believe that God's view of salvation is much larger.

The Greek word *sozo* that is translated save has a much broader meaning. It can mean everything from healing, to deliverance, to preserving from natural dangers, to spiritual covering. It can even mean a deliverance from trouble in such a way that the trouble never arrives. God doesn't have to wait for the hour of crisis for His salvation to come. He can look ahead and prevent the hour of crisis!

In the book of James, the Spirit is addressing Christians when He admonishes them to "receive with meekness the implanted word, which is able to save your souls" (James 1:21b). When God thinks of salvation, I do not believe that He is simply wanting to enlist another name for the kingdom. He is interested in salvation. He is interested in a complete deliverance! Certainly one of the greatest deliverances is a deliverance from hell. But He doesn't enjoy seeing us go through *any* unnecessary pain. He wants us to fully receive His Word and avoid as much heartache as possible. Every deliverance is important to Him and not just deliverance from a judgment to hell.

His own purpose statement in Luke 4 includes healing the "brokenhearted", proclaiming liberty to the "captives" and the "oppressed", and giving sight to the "blind". Each of those is a candidate for "salvation" according to the broader definition. Just because someone is enrolled into the kingdom (saved eternally), does not mean that they are not candidates for more of His focus of love to receive further salvation.

He truly is a helper of the helpless. "Pure religion" (James 1:27) is to visit the widows and the orphans. He wants to bring His salvation wherever it is needed, whenever it is needed to all of His brethren, whether "saved" (Christians) or unsaved (non-Christians). In fact, I am not sure that there is as much distinction between the Christian and non-Christian in the mind of God as we would like to create.

All of us need His salvation continually. Certainly the justice of God demands that there be a difference between the treatment of the sinner and the saved, but it is the nature of the heart of God to love everyone and to desire for all to come to salvation.

Without question, the *greatest* salvation needed is restoration of relationship with a holy God. Without that, what is a physical healing really worth? Without that, who cares if the troubles of this life are taken away? We must put first priority on those who have the greatest need. We must set as our highest goal to reach the spiritually lost or we will shrink back into the comfortable zone of mutual gratification with other Christians and seek a "salvation" of other believers from trouble.

However, if we can keep our heart beat on helping those that cannot return the favor, I do believe that there is value in being a priest of God's salvation wherever it is needed, ignoring the distinction between the "lost" and the "saved." After all, do we really know who is saved and who is lost spiritually? It is very possible that in by-passing one that we think to be saved, we may be missing one of the most needy persons.

One of the most helpful instructions I ever received about witnessing was to "treat the unsaved just like you would the saved." What does that mean? When we are with believers, we will often talk about answered prayers or concepts from the Word or other kinds of spiritual things. As soon as we get around the lost, we often assume that they will not respond to these kinds of things and we completely censor our language so that we don't "offend" the lost person and lose our chance to win him to God.

We may actually be ahead to treat the "lost" just like the "saved." If someone that was "saved" needed a job, what would we do? We would openly pray for him to get a job. Why should it be any different with the "lost"? Many times, answered prayer is the greatest evangelistic tool we have, but we have to pray the prayer for the perceived need openly with the person before we have the chance to pray with him to receive Jesus.

Taking it one step further, I know of many Christians that are out of fellowship with God. Have they lost their salvation? Are they backslidden and hanging on by a thread? Are they eternally saved but just losing some of their reward? Does any of that really matter? They need "salvation." They need their relationship with God restored. They need Romans 8:16 to become reality in their lives, to know that God's Spirit is present and active in their lives and that they are truly a loved child of God. They need His "salvation." God's heart is crying out to them as one that is lost from His fold. He leaves the 99 to go searching. He wants present fellowship with His own.

Is it really any different dealing with the unsaved? They do not need to be treated as some entirely different group that might give us leprosy unless we get them saved. We need to speak of the things of Christ and pray openly and simply restore fellowship with the Father for them as well.

Many times, the ones witnessing out of a duty orientation may have almost as great a need for restoration of fellowship with the Father as the "lost" ones they are targeting. How can we give away what we do not even have? Setting up distinctions of achievements like "saved", "sanctified", or "Spirit filled" may actually deny a present reality of current relationship. Salvation is not a one-time act performed to achieve heaven. It is the opening of a door to an ongoing relationship with Jesus Christ through the Holy Spirit.

The real question is, "Today, right now, am I living in His salvation?" Today, the lost person needs His salvation. Today, the saved person needs His salvation. Though our eternal destiny may be different, on a given day the saved person's level of fellowship with God may be very little different than the lost. We still need His goodness today. We simply need to share the goodness that has been shared with us.

Entering His Heart

To enter His heart, we need to move into acts of service for others that He has called us to do, especially acts that cause us to love those outside of our normal circle of love.

There are three important keys. First, we do have to do something. Many of the spiritual disciplines can be done segregated away in a closet. If we are not careful, we create an image of the spiritual person as being someone mystical, hidden away, and walking in some sort of weird invisible life. Love is not love until it is expressed. Great intentions don't cut it. A spiritual man is not a spiritual man until he responds spiritually. He does not have a heart for the lost until he opens his mouth or extends his hand. God may have given him everything he needs on the inside to do the job through prayer, but until he acts, it is nothing.

However, action in and of itself is not the answer. Jesus said that "the Son can do nothing of Himself, but what He sees the

Father do; for whatever He does, the Son also does in like manner" (John 6:19b). Jesus did not even trust Himself to step out and randomly begin to shower forth His love on whoever happened to pass by. Jesus had to enter into the heart of the Father.

That is where the spiritual disciplines do help. We have nothing to give anyone unless the Father blesses what we do. Have you ever told someone that the presence of God would come to them according to Romans 8:16 only to have absolutely nothing happen? Was the Kingdom helped or hindered? Maybe your solution was to never be vulnerable by offering God's presence again and from that point on you chose to take the safe way out and simply pray a prayer with them and tell them that God had done something. In some cases, this can lead to a false assurance of salvation if the person is simply not "with you" or "with God" in the prayer. Many people cooperate in a sinner's prayer just to be nice, or even to get rid of us, but have no experience of His salvation. How do we know the difference?

Prayer hopefully has put us back in touch with a real and living God. We have a sense of His presence and His speaking. We are sensitive to the fact that someone is going to be coming across our path that needs encouragement. Our eyes are open and when the person shows up, like Jesus, we do what our Father has shown us to do. Entering God's heart is not just performing random acts of kindness. It can be as specific as the most delicate incisions of a surgeon's hand.

There may be times when His guidance is more general. James tells us that "Therefore, to him who knows to do good and does not do it, to him it is sin" (James 4:17). In the parable explaining who is our neighbor, two "spiritual" men walked right past the need. Only the supposedly less spiritual Samaritan stopped to help. We must have an eye toward helping others all the time and in all situations.

However, we are not always equipped to do the job, nor is the person on the other end always ready to receive the help. Our predisposition should be to serve, but we must also check it out with the Father. At times, He may stay our hand from helping. That is almost dangerous to even say, as the selfish will use it as an excuse. Yet what do the selfish really have to give anyway? They can offer only human help and human compassion. We need to be about the business of offering God's help and God's compassion, which can only be done if we have been in touch with Him and have received what we need to give to a situation.

The final part of moving into His heart is getting outside of ourselves. Some of our service (or ministry) may be done among those that we know and love. Again, we must do what we see the Father doing. However, lest our own hearts deceive us, we need to have a constant eye on a group other than our own. That is what missions is all about. It is loving someone that we have no inherent reason to love. It is keeping our focus over there on purpose because we know that we will tend to do enough for us and ours.

Again, this can be taken too far. We can totally neglect our own. That too is a mistake. That too must be regulated by the Father. It is not spiritual to neglect self or family. Many times that simply destroys our potential for taking His love to the ones He wanted us to minister to.

But I do believe that His greatest love is displayed when we allow His love to funnel through us in a situation when there is absolutely no human reason to love. Sometimes this can mean loving a son or daughter that has been absolutely unlovable. Sometimes it means going to the ends of the earth to share the gospel with someone that we have never seen or hardly even heard about. His love is radical and it doesn't meet the standard of good human sense.

He is a Father

When God describes Himself as a Father, it is not just a metaphor. He is in truth a Father of a very, very large family. And like any good father, His love expands to each and every child that is born. When one hurts, He knows it. When one rejoices, He knows it. The love of this Father is not limited to a select few of His chosen ones.

Imagine, even for a moment, what it must be like to be a Father to all of humanity. He cannot become calloused and hard toward the pain that He sees. It is not in His nature. His love for the children doesn't shut down temporarily just to make it easier to deal with the hardness that is in man's heart.

On the contrary, His heart remains soft and loving. How do we know that? Very simple. All of heaven rejoices when one sinner repents. And heaven takes its cues from the Father. The Father leaves the 99 to go get the one that is lost. And there is great rejoicing when the one is found. His heart must still be soft and loving. He is still crying out for all of humanity, for all of His children.

Will you enter into the heart of the Father? Can you, for even a moment, begin to think like the God and Father of us all? Can you see what He sees? Can you let Him move you to the place or to the person that He has His eye on? Certainly the heart of the Father knows when one of His children is ready to receive His help. We live in such a limited scope, with such a selfish and small world. He is a Father, with an incredible love for all His children. And He asks us to come, enter into His heart. What a privilege! What an honor! What a life!

It is possible to do all the right things and never enter His heart. Love is the greatest standard. Human love is eclipsed by the standard the Father had when He sent Christ, His only begotten Son, to die for us. Now He beckons to His other children. Will any of them enter into that kind of love?

Can we at least take the first step of obedience to serve others and see where it leads? The Father waits with open arms, wanting to reveal more of His heart to any that will become a vessel of His love for His children. Enter the heart of the Father!

II Kings 4:1-7

A certain woman of the wives of the sons of the prophets cried out to Elisha, saying, "Your servant my husband is dead, and you know that your servant feared the LORD. And the creditor is coming to take my two sons to be his slaves."

So Elisha said to her, "What shall I do for you? Tell me, what do you have in the house?" And she said, "Your maidservant has nothing in the house but a jar of oil."

Then he said, "Go, borrow vessels from everywhere, from all your neighbors-- empty vessels; do not gather just a few.

And when you have come in, you shall shut the door behind you and your sons; then pour it into all those vessels, and set aside the full ones.

So she went from him and shut the door behind her and her sons, who brought the vessels to her; and she poured it out.

Now it came to pass, when the vessels were full, that she said to her son, "Bring me another vessel." And he said to her, "There is not another vessel." So the oil ceased.

Then she came and told the man of God. And he said, "Go, sell the oil and pay your debt; and you and your sons live on the rest."

Chapter 21

Understanding God's Ways

My District Superintendent shared with me a story about a woman who was approaching her 101st birthday. At the close of the service, she came forward in response to an invitation to come for prayer. Expecting some physical need, the Superintendent bent forward to hear the request. "I just want more of Jesus!" Her voice was little more than a whisper, but had a fervor unmatched in all the congregation.

Going deeper in God truly is a life study. It may be the only life long study that will keep our interest year after year. It is definitely a study that we will never fully master, as we continue to strive to become fully like God.

The story in 2 Kings 4 gives us a picture of the purpose this life holds for each one of us. The woman in the story is in a helpless situation. Her two sons are about to be sold as slaves as a result of the death of her husband, who had been one of the prophets, a servant of God. She does the only thing she knows to do. She cries out to the man of God.

The woman herself is a broken and empty vessel. She seemingly has nothing left, only a "jar of oil" in the house. As she humbles herself before the man of God, it is that jar of oil that becomes the starting point.

Elisha tells her to collect empty vessels from her neighbors and adds "do not gather just a few." When the door is shut, she begins to pour from the one nearly empty vessel into the empty vessels, and the oil does not run out until the last vessel is full. The woman could have left that room rich, if she had only gathered enough vessels. As it was, she still had a more than adequate supply to meet her needs.

Common Vessels or Collectors of God?

Though this is not an "interpretation" of the story, I believe that this story provides us with a picture of how God uses this life to complete His purposes in us. Each of us, in our own way is a broken and empty vessel. At times, we may have some dirty water or some other thing of little value in us. The common vessels were used to carry all sorts of things.

In the larger picture, it is the will of God to fill each one of us with His oil, with the presence of His Holy Spirit. Without His presence, each of us is just a cheap, common vessel, possibly broken or empty or full of dirty water. With His oil, we become something of real value.

Yet, this picture can be taken one step farther. How do we collect jars of oil in our lives? The answer is simple: we collect the oil in common clay jars through the common events of our lives. The verses in Deuteronomy 6 that explain how to love the Lord our God with all our heart, strength, mind, and soul are very explicit. We include God in all the normal daily things of life like eating, at bedtime, when we are traveling, or through deliberate education.

Each of these events of life becomes a vessel that potentially could hold more oil. Yet each of these events is only a common vessel in itself. It is of little or no value unless it is somehow filled with the oil. If the oil is poured into many vessels, we could become very rich spiritually speaking. If it is only poured into a few, we remain comparatively pour.

Our daily habits and activities become the most important "vessels" of our lives. It is possible for our "vessels" to be filled with dirty water, perhaps full of germs and sickness. Many of our daily lives include things that would be considered "sickness" before God and yet we continue to walk in them day after day.

God's first purpose is to empty the vessel. He does not want to mix His oil with dirty water. The woman herself had become an empty vessel. In total brokenness, she appealed to the man of God. She no longer had anything of herself to depend upon. She had no choice. She was empty. She had to appeal to God.

So often, when we see continual pain and heartache, God's purpose is very simple: He is trying to empty the vessel. It is His goal to pour in the oil, but He will not do so without being asked. And He will not do so on the terms of a stubborn and strong-willed person. He will only do it on His terms: a request from a broken and empty vessel. He will not allow His oil to glorify a proud vessel that thinks itself to be the reason for the accumulation of the oil. He waits for the broken and empty request.

Every day of our lives is a collection of many vessels. Our thought life could be compared to a vessel. If our thought life is continually on things of this world like "What shall I eat, drink, or wear?" it is already full. There is no room for His oil. If it is on things that are sick and disgusting, it is full of dirty and diseased water. His oil is not available. There must be an emptying and a cleansing. The blood of Jesus cleansing our minds is our only hope.

Becoming a Candidate for God's Blessing

The first step is to make room for the things of God. We must stop the busyness of our minds as well as our wicked thoughts. Until we do, there simply is no room for the thoughts of God. We must empty the vessel called our thought life.

The next step is to begin to purposely integrate the thoughts about God into our lives. Once we begin this habit, we have a clean vessel in a shape that will possibly hold the oil of God, but we are not yet complete. At this point, we are still vulnerable to pride in our own accomplishments. Thinking the right thoughts is good, but we still need to recognize the need for His oil to make the thought life what it ought to be.

Psalm 127 says:

> Unless the LORD builds the house, they labor in vain who build it; unless the LORD guards the city, the watchman stays awake in vain.

It is vain for you to rise up early, to sit up late, to eat the bread of sorrows; for so He gives His beloved sleep.

A man can set out to build a house, and that is a good thing. A guard can guard a city, and that too is a good thing. Yet, if the blessing of God is not on that particular activity, it will fail. Extra effort, rising early and staying up late, will have no positive effect. Either God blesses the activity or it is doomed to failure.

A man can set out to build up a thought life that is pleasing to God, and that is a good thing. Yet if the blessing of God is not on that activity, it will fail. And why would the blessing of God not be on the man who was trying to build a thought life about the things of God?

The answer comes back to having an empty vessel. The man, who with great pride, sets out to be the "best" in the Scriptures, will not have the blessing of God. The man who humbles himself and recognizes that he needs the anointing of the Holy Spirit to teach him, as 1 John 2:27 promises, will have the blessing of the Lord.

In a way, the thought life becomes one of the vessels that can hold the oil of God. If the thought life is cleansed and focused on God, it is a candidate to be filled. But it must first recognize its need for help and call upon the Lord continually for more of His oil. Only then does the thought life truly reflect the truth of God.

This takes us all the way back to the first chapters of the book. To reflect truth, we must illustrate to the world that we cannot function apart from God. We were designed to be continually sustained by His presence, by His oil. The person who thinks that his thoughts about God are adequate in themselves is not reflecting truth. To illustrate truth, a person must continually depend on the Holy Spirit to guide and direct his thoughts, even when those thoughts are purposely upon Scripture and on God. (One might even say especially when those thoughts are upon Scripture and on God.)

Each area of our life is a vessel. Our Bible reading is a vessel. Our thought life is a vessel. Our church attendance is a vessel. Our service is a vessel. Our fasting is a vessel. Our time spent in work is a vessel. Our relationships are a vessel. Our outreach is a vessel. Each of those vessels must first be clean and then be filled with the oil of His anointing. When each of these areas is a vessel full of His oil, we become a true reflection of truth.

This is the purpose of God in each and every situation. Certainly many evil things happen in and around us. Our own families are often victims of some of the results of sin. The heartache that sin causes, along with the resulting punishments on the human race of sickness and death, simply cannot be erased by God. To do so would mean that He is no longer just.

Yet in every situation, He is at work to bring about His will. He is at work to bring about clean vessels that are full of His oil, reflecting the original purpose of their creation. He does not just want good works. He wants works filled with His presence and goodness, that bring glory to Him.

Digging Deeper

In the story just before the widow with the vessels, Elisha had been called to the aid of the armies of Judah, Israel, and Edom.

Elisha instructed the armies to dig ditches throughout the valley according to the Word of the Lord. The digging of the ditches was to be an act of faith. The Lord told them that the ditches would be filled with water, satisfying their thirst.

Again, we see a picture of our lives. If we are to know the blessing of the Lord, we too must act in faith to "dig ditches." Those ditches represent the very habits and disciplines that we establish in our lives. They become the container for the water from God that is about to fall. The ditches themselves are nothing. The habits themselves are nothing. Without the water, ditches only represent human effort. With the water, they represent a reward for our faith toward God. With the anointing oil, the habits become a holding place for the things of God.

Many people try to dig ditches at any place of their own choosing. Can you imagine if these same armies had tried digging ditches the next time they got in trouble? It would have been sheer folly. We need to dig ditches at the direction of the Lord. We need to build our habits and our disciplines at the direction of the Lord. No disciplines mean that the blessing of the Lord will simply run off the land. Disciplines of our own choosing will result in a tired, burned out person who sees no results. We must be led by God in the choosing of our disciplined activities toward God and then we must also call upon the Lord for His anointing in those activities.

The "ditches" story has one more picture that adds to our understanding. To the enemy, the water in the ditches looked like blood. In this case, the enemy thought that the three armies must have attacked each other and came running to what they thought would be a slaughter. They ended up being the ones that were slaughtered. With the refreshing of the water that had accumulated in the ditches, the three armies were too much for the enemy Moabites.

At times when we follow the way of the anointing, we too appear to be easy targets for the enemy. The outside world thinks that we are crazy and that we are losing our own blood in the process. What the world doesn't realize is that the blood of Jesus is our supply. It is our refreshing. His death on the cross provides the flow of water that refreshes us. And when the enemy attacks, if we have been truly refreshed by His flow, the enemy becomes easy prey for us. The thing Satan meant for evil, God turns to the good.

Unfortunately, many of us have not taken the time to dig ditches. Can you imagine what would have happened if the three armies had not dug the ditches? Wasted with thirst, they would have been easy prey for the Moabite army.

The church today is in much the same state. We have not dug ditches. We do not know our Bibles. We do not continually pray. We are not in close fellowship with one another. We do not have a heart to reach out to those that are unlike us. We do not have the basic kinds of obedience and godly behavior established as habits in our lives. We are easy prey.

Vessels of Life to a Captive World

It is God's will for the church to be an overcoming force, but that will never happen until some of the basic disciplines are firmly established. Boot camp must come before the battle. Other parts of God's body have established themselves in the disciplines but are failing to depend on the oil of God's presence.

They are armies dying with thirst. The disciplines are the vessels; God's presence keeps the vessels (or the ditches) full.

We see tragedy happen, and we wonder why. If our ditches had been dug and full of water, the enemy would have been the prey. Instead, God watches with a heavy heart as we are destroyed and listens with a grieved heart as we blame Him for not protecting us.

There is much heartache in the world. Sin rages and the church seems powerless to do anything about it. Many have fallen by the wayside, wondering why God did nothing to stop the raging torrent of evil, all the while not recognizing the same raging torrent within themselves. Had the vessels been cleansed and filled, the outcome could have been much different.

Jesus can turn the dirty water of our vessels into wine, just as He did at the wedding feast of Cana. Each vessel that is fully given to Him, He will instantly change, but we hold many vessels back, and we guard others. It is so difficult to let go. It is so difficult to let growth come. It scares us and we prefer to hang on to the little bit of oil that we have.

Growth is normal. Going deeper in God will happen if you only cooperate with God. Begin to dig some ditches. Find the basic lifestyle in Christ that God is calling you to. Fervently seek the renewing and strengthening presence of God. These are the food and water of growth. It is really quite simple. Even a child can understand it.

God wants you. He wants you to be a vessel of His presence. He wants you to be the image of His life. With His help, the basics can be set in order and then He can begin to shine in you the way He wants to. And He can use you to touch His family, your brethren, the ones He sees hurting and in need.

Have you ever seen the glow of a newborn baby? The stamp of His life is all over child after child. Have you ever seen the glow of a 100-year-old? In many ways it is even more glorious . . . unless of course the darkness has stamped out the glory. God hates that. And so should we.

What in this world is more precious than the glow of the glory of God? We let bitterness become more important . . . and hatreds . . . and jealousies . . . and lusts . . . . Are you glowing now with His presence? Then you are growing, growing deeper in Christ. Has sin shrouded His presence? Then His purpose is not being fulfilled in your life.

Satan has set out to stamp out the glory of God wherever he finds it, and that especially includes you as a believer. If you let him, he will take the spoil from you. If you begin to dig ditches, you will take the spoil from him. After all, we are the ones who are to pillage the gates of hell. We are the ones who are to go into his domain and bring out those in bondage and to see the light and glory of God released into them.

Satan knows that and he will try to keep you weak. It should not be, but it can be if you do not put first things first.

Learn from the babies. They know enough to cry out for food. Learn from the 100-year-old woman. She too knew enough to cry out for real food. Jesus said, "My food is to do the will of Him, Who sent Me, and to finish His work" (John 4:34b). When what we want most is more of Jesus, we too will go deeper in God. May God bless you in your journey!

Chapter 22

WHY?

Why?

It is the one question that won't go away. Life isn't fair! It is Peter looking at John at the end of John's gospel, asking, "Why not him instead of me?" It is Judas asking, "Why couldn't Jesus have been the military strong man I had hoped for?" It is the people of the newly formed churches asking, "Why must Paul go to Jerusalem to be imprisoned and to suffer when he could be here ministering to us?"

Why? If we are not careful, it is *the* question that will destroy us! It causes us to compare ourselves among ourselves and that is not wise (2 Cor. 10:12). It gives rise to self-pity and a whole list of other destructive self-seekings.

The bottom line is the desire of God's heart for intimacy with us and our desperate need for deep intimacy with Him. He desires that more than anything else. We need that more than anything else. It is His greatest goal.

The athlete in training who is looking for the championship edge pays a very dear price. If he or she begins to look around, that edge is lost. Self-gratification begins to win out. The championship is lost.

It is no different in the spiritual realm. The title of this book is
<u>Going Deeper</u>.   It is designed for those who want the
championship edge in the spiritual realm. When James and John
asked for an "edge" in the kingdom, Jesus answered with a
question: "Are you able to drink the cup that I am about to
drink, and be baptized with the baptism that I am baptized
with?" (Matt. 20:22b).

The question is simple: On a daily basis, will you pay the price?
Many will answer "No" to that question. Jesus tells us that the
way is "narrow" and those that find it will be "few."   And
because many choose not to respond, there will be a much
greater suffering among humanity than would have been if the
righteous had stepped up and taken their place. And then, many
will see the suffering and ask "Why?"

But many times, I do see the suffering of the one that does step
up and ask "Why?" I thought God had good things for those
that followed Him. I thought that God would cause even the
enemies of the righteous to be at peace with him. I thought God
came to wipe every tear . . . and He does.

But Jesus also tells us that just as the world persecuted Him, so
it would persecute us. Just as it hated and misunderstood Him,
so it would hate and misunderstand us. Just as He suffered to
partake of His glory, so must we.

Beginning to See an Answer

How can we possibly reconcile the good and the bad? It makes
no sense . . . until you begin to focus primarily on the spiritual
realm. What happened *to* Job seems senseless, until you focus

on what happened *in* Job. He went from being ritualistic and fearful of what might happen to being humbled and full of awe for God.

While the natural consequences may seem extremely unfair, the spiritual realm is both immediate and absolutely fair. The one who holds bitterness will be instantly changed in spirit to reflect the image of bitterness. The one who receives forgiveness from God is also instantly changed and has a freedom and a release on the inside.

The one who focuses on the natural realm cannot help but become bitter and frustrated because "life just isn't fair." What God will calls us to walk through seems extremely unfair . . . because He calls us to walk right into the death of the flesh. The very things we fear, the very things we do not want to have to deal with, the very things we do not want to give up, those will be the things that He will challenge. The very person that is so repulsive to us, that is the one that He will call us to minister to.

Why? Because He must be our God for us to reflect truth. He must be our God for us to have freedom in the inner man. He must be our God for us to have life uninterrupted. If there is someone we fear, if there is someone we hate, that someone can step between us and God. His flow can be interrupted.

As Romans 8 tells us, nothing can interrupt the flow of the life and love of God into our inner man as long as we are "under the Spirit," as long as we are keeping our focus on Him. In most cases, pain causes us to lose our focus, which in turn brings an immediate negative change in our inner man, which in turn causes us to question and doubt God. Hopefully, the person soon realizes what has happened and seeks restoration with the Spirit of God. Often, the previous spiritual flow has been so meager that the removal of His presence is not even noticed.

Becoming a Virtuoso

It is like that with a championship athlete or a virtuoso. Take away one day of practice and the virtuoso can tell you that he has lost the edge. Take away two days of practice, and other virtuosos will notice. Go three days without practice and the whole world will notice.

The amateur can go out and pick up a basketball and be "up to par" in just a few minutes. The amateur can sit down at the piano and be "back up to speed" with just a little work. The virtuoso cannot.

In the same way, those that dabble in spiritual things will have a sense of pride and accomplishment over some minor sensing of the Spirit's flow. Yet, take away the practice, take away the presence, and they will hardly notice the difference. Following the "rudder" of God's peace is little protection to that person, since there is so little difference between having God's peace and not having God's peace. For the virtuoso in spirit, the difference is great and so is the protection from falling into sin.

The flow of the Spirit is absolutely fair and just. It can be very cruel on the flesh (the tendency to satisfy self instead of God), since God knows that to be a real virtuoso in spirit, the flesh must die. In the midst of a death experience, we often turn our eyes away from God to the pain, and then our spirit dries up. The seeming "torment from God" is doubly cruel. Yet it is our own spirit's choice to focus on the pain that allows the "death to the flesh" to become a "torment."

If we do not turn away from God, there is a flow of God's comfort and peace that offsets and indeed overcomes the pain of death to self. Unfortunately, staying focused on God during a time of turmoil is much easier said than done.

Though things of the spirit are immediate, it is also important to note that the presence of the Spirit will not always be joy and peace. At times it may be a quiet sense of patience or even a subtle compassion. At other times, any sensation of the Spirit may seem to come to an end. The Spirit distances Himself, offering only the most slight impression of His presence. At this point, it is easy to focus only on the pain and to think that He has completely withdrawn His presence.

However, if we value even these subtle touches from Him and respond with a longing for more of Him, our spiritual sensitivity will actually increase! It is like turning a gauge from measuring in kilowatts to measuring in watts. The end result will be a new level of openness to the flow of the Spirit.

During the difficult times, it is easy to feel lost and perhaps begin to think that God is disciplining us for some sin. His presence seems to be far from us. It is as if we have been banished from Him. It is not unlike an athlete who begins to stretch himself beyond his normal workout. The muscles begin to ache and the whole body may begin to convulse in complaint. The body would seem to be saying, "This is doing no good at all! In fact, if anything it is doing damage." Yet, over a period of time, the athlete steps up to a new level of performance.

In the same way, God's goal is a bountiful supply of the Spirit to each and every one of us. That is why Jesus suffered and died, so that the Spirit might be freely shed abroad to whosoever would desire. And that bountiful supply ultimately depends upon us keeping our spirit open toward Him.

The one that turns toward the pain and becomes bitter shuts down the flow of grace. The one that tunes in his spiritual sensitivity gauge to be attentive to even the seemingly slight spiritual flow maintains a sense of God's touch and enlarges the flow of His grace.

It is like the championship athlete that must learn to ignore the cries of the body that are related to the intense training (and yet is able to distinguish the cry that would point to an injury). The focus of the athlete must be on the end goal of championship performance.

In the same way, as Satan comes with every assault he can mount against God's best, the virtuoso in spirit must learn to focus on God's end. He must turn up the spiritual sensitivity gauge until the experience of the love of God is still a reality even amidst the most difficult of times. He must continue to walk by faith in the middle of a flow of God's grace, even when all the feelings of the natural man are screaming that the love of God has departed.

When a man or woman can still focus on the slight spiritual flow amidst Satan's greatest all out attack, God has a warrior that will not be shaken. He has a virtuoso in spirit that is "under the Spirit" and thus will live in a continual experience of God's love just as Romans 8 describes.

God must take steps to increase abundance by increasing our sensitivity. During these growth seasons, our prayer life, our devotional life, and our obedience will be stretched. It would be easy to turn away and not be sensitive to His touch. But His grace is sufficient.

And with the stretching comes a humbling of self that brings a greater grace. And with more grace comes more abundance. And that is something to celebrate. The flow of His presence is nearing the point of being a sure thing, till suddenly it seems to be gone and there is no reason for it. Why?

Creating Capacity for More of Christ

At times a spiritual dryness or discomfort does sets in, and even at our most sensitive setting, the Spirit seems to be gone. It is very important for us not to automatically assume that this discomfort or dryness is the result of some sin. It may simply be the Lord wanting to develop a greater capacity in us.

Anytime we think it may be sin, we should ask God to convict us of any needed areas. If we ask Him to bring to light the hidden sins, He is well able to surface any sin that He is wanting to deal with. And if He surfaces it, we will not be able to ignore the graphic way He demonstrates our sin to us! We will see our own sin as we have never seen it before! If nothing surfaces, we should wait patiently before Him to lead us into deeper levels.

The vessel that God is to use mightily must be completely His. In Leviticus, the offering that was symbolic of a man or woman completely given to God was the burnt offering. This offering was not a sin offering. Leviticus 5:11b describes a grain offering for sin saying, "He shall put no oil on it, nor shall he put frankincense on it for it is a sin offering." The oil, symbolic of the presence of God's Spirit, and the sweet aroma of the frankincense were not allowed in a sin offering, but were required for a burnt offering.

To prepare the burnt offering, the priests would very carefully wash the animal. It was to be clean before it was to be offered. The symbolism is clear. Sin has already been taken care of by a sin offering. The sacrifice is washed and is clean. The sacrifice that is about to take place is not to cleanse something, but yet is still described in one place as having "atoning" value.

If it is not a sin offering, how can it have atoning value? In the burnt offering, the priests would first wash and then burn every bit of the animal until only ashes remained. This is our picture of complete consecration to God. It is a picture of the first commandment being completely fulfilled, with nothing held back. It is atoning because it is an appropriate sacrifice and service to God. Just as the sin offering presented God's people clean, the burnt offering presented His people as fulfilling the proper sacrifice and service to Him. In several places, He declares the burnt offering to be a "sweet aroma."

The New Testament parallel is to be a living sacrifice (Rom. 12:1), wholly consumed for God "which is our reasonable service." As a people of God, we have focused on whether or not we are in sin. The burnt offering shifts the focus to being completely consumed for righteousness sake.

This offering is about loving the Lord our God with all our heart, mind, soul, and strength. To become a burnt offering is to be a "sweet aroma to the Lord" (Lev. 2:13b) even as the incense of Jesus' life was continually a sweet aroma to God. To be a burnt offering is to be totally consumed with pleasing the Father just as Jesus was. It is not about sin needing to be burned off. That was taken care of by the sin offering. It is about total sacrifice to God.

In the same way, the Spirit comes to consecrate us to God. We immediately think that we are in sin. We feel the fire of His burning consuming us and we declare that His presence has departed from us. We "know" that He has left us because it feels so unlike anytime when His presence is flowing. But we are wrong. The fire of His consecration has begun. He is consuming any part of us that would diminish His capacity to flow through us. It is not an elimination of sin, but a call to further consecration, a call that says "Will you pay the price with Me to reach out as a vessel of life to your brothers?"

To those who have seen its results, the time of the fire of consecration is no longer a hated thing, but a thing of great value. It is **the** thing that can ultimately increase our capacity for more of Him. It is hard to recognize and even harder to cooperate with the fire, but one of our precious promises is that we would be "baptized with the Holy Spirit and *fire*" (Luke 3:16b).

To the one focused on the natural man, it is not worth it. To the one who wants a capacity in Him, it is not even a choice worth a second thought. "Press on" is the heart cry of the Paul's of the world. For them, a greater capacity for God is the very essence of life, the fullness of life to be sought after.

Unfortunately, this life can be difficult to see when the smoke of the burnt offering rises all around us, and suddenly we realize we are the ones on fire. We are the ones burning. At this point, the natural man tries to take over and to declare that the Spirit has departed. Of course He hasn't, but any sense His presence has for all practical purposes vanished, even for the spiritually sensitive.

It is a season of consecration. It is a season of dedicating the vessel completely so that the flow of His Spirit might ultimately be increased. This is not to be confused with discipline for sin, but is a time of God asking, "How much will you give me?" It is a time of increasing the capacity of the believer for more of Him.

I'm reminded of the statement in folklore that "In absence the heart grows fonder." To the one that truly loves God, and stays focused on Him, the season of consecration is a time of "absence" but also of greatly increasing hunger and thirst for God. During the fire itself, the hunger and thirst may not be noticed. But as the fire begins to subside, the appetite surfaces and the heart has an overwhelming desire for more of Him. The seeming absence of the Spirit, in combination with the fire has done its work.

God responds to the hunger by pouring out His grace. More grace means more capacity. And more capacity means more flow of His grace (unless we are in a season of consecration!).

Once we understand the capacity delays, life really is fair at the spiritual level. The world may trash us, but nothing can "separate us from the love of God which is in Christ Jesus our Lord" (Rom. 8:39b). Only our own turning away and attending to our own flesh can eclipse our very present experience of His love. (It doesn't end the love, just the experience of it!).

Increase or Decrease?

It is also very important to recognize that a deeper walk with God cannot be comparative. If we set out to have the best prayer life of anyone we know, we will surely be disappointed. If our heart desires to be the most serving, loving, or considerate, someone with an even stronger love is sure to surface.

Going deeper in Christ simply means enlarging the flow of His Spirit in us. As John the Baptist said of Christ, "He must increase, but I must decrease" (John 3:30). John did not try to compete. He couldn't, and neither can we. There will always be someone else who is "deeper."

Comparison cannot be the goal. If you must, compare yourself with what you were a year ago. Yet, even here, there is the pitfall of developing pride over how far you have come. Take a lesson from John the Baptist. Die to self and live to God.

Decrease without letting it bother you. Comparison, by its very nature, is self-centered. If you really do want to increase His flow in you, you must die to self and all things that feed the self.

At times, you may feel like you really aren't making any progress, and you will be tempted to try to find some signposts. Trust God! If you are focused on Him, He is at work. You don't need to be able to see the progress with your own eyes.

In fact, some of the people who are growing the most, have some of the greatest doubts about their own growth. Why? Because they are more aware of their sin than ever! In the very times when you feel like you are doing the worst, you may be doing the best!

So how do I know how I am doing? Even asking that question borders on trouble, since it focuses on self. But if you must know, ask God (1 Cor. 4:3-4). He will show you. And ask a few close, godly friends. They too will know. And if they are a true friend, they will speak the truth to you.

It is best, though, to stay focused on God. Forget about levels attained. Concentrate on His call for today. Enjoy His blessing for today. Live in this world, but not of this world.

Remember that the natural things are given to us to enhance the spiritual. Habits of Bible reading and prayer make it easy for our spirits to stay in a flow with God. Events that happen shock us and bring us back to an awareness of our need for God.

Even the routine things of life give us the chance to make a habit of the presence of God and to continually sow more and more of His image into our inner man. Everything we do can begin to play a supporting role in our walk with God. Life is meant to be the vessel that molds and shapes us into His image!

A Calling Beyond All Cost Considerations

Yet this life is much more than the sum of a bunch of actions we do. It is a bringing forth of the image of Christ into this world. It is establishing the righteousness of God in Christ that He has already purchased for us and provided for us. It is receiving of the divine goodness in the invisible realm, so that it might be made known to all in the natural realm. It is being a brother to Jesus and a part of His body. It is a touching of the "brethren" of Christ.

It is an incredibly high calling. It is a challenge that we can never fully conquer, and yet in our pressing forward to conquer, we are declared perfect because previous imperfections are washed away by the blood of Christ.

It is the highest of callings, far beyond that of the angels. It is to be of Christ and like Christ. It is to be in partnership with God. When put in that perspective, some of the once huge trials don't seem so large any more. Jesus is worth it! Life in the Spirit really is fair after all!

If you've ever wondered if it was worth the cost, look to that 100 year old woman. Look to Moses. Look to David. The cost of walking with God can be great, but how does it compare with the cost of even minor sins in the great men of God?

The wages of sin truly is death. We see it in Absalom, Adonijah, and even Solomon as David's sins are so evident in the next generation. The price tag of sin is so incredibly high. How can we even begin to compare any sacrifice we could make for God to the price of sin?

Jacob loved a woman, Rachel, in so great a way that seven years of servitude for her seemed as only a few days. How much more should we be able to love the God of this universe that sent His Son to die for us, and Who also blesses us with His great and continual love? If our love is truly great, the sacrifice is no longer a sacrifice!

Why? The question no longer is relevant. The sacrifice is worth it!

Are you now ready to pay the price? Are you ready for His flow in you to be so great that it would be very difficult for you to stumble? That is the essence of 2 Peter 1:4-10:

> But also for this very reason, giving all diligence, add to your faith virtue, to virtue knowledge, to knowledge self-control, to self-control perseverance, to perseverance godliness, to godliness brotherly kindness, and to brotherly kindness love.
>
> For if these things are yours and abound, you will be neither barren nor unfruitful in the knowledge of our Lord Jesus Christ. For he who lacks these things is shortsighted, even to blindness, and has forgotten that he was cleansed from his old sins.
>
> Therefore, brethren, be even more diligent to make your call and election sure, for if you do these things you will never stumble; for so an entrance will be supplied to you abundantly into the everlasting kingdom of our Lord and Savior Jesus Christ.

Are you ready for an abundant entrance into the kingdom? Then why wait? Jesus tells us, "Blessed are the poor in spirit for theirs *is* the kingdom of heaven." If you are truly ready to die to self, and to follow after the principles of the Word, today is your day to begin.

The fountains of heaven are open to replenish the spirits of the thirsty, to satisfy the desires of the hungry, and to abundantly bless the hearts of the humble.

At the cost of death, will you answer the call to go deeper? All heaven awaits your answer!

About the Author

Especially from the college years on, David A. Case has had a passion to get to know the Scriptures, but even more to know the God of the Scriptures. From leading peer Bible studies in college, to reaching out to fellow teachers and to students as a public school teacher, he has desired to be a positive Christian influence on those around him. First as a lay person, and later as an associate pastor and then a pastor, he has continued to walk in and encourage others to walk in a life of accountability to God and to other believers.

Being especially moved by the pain and dysfunction of Modern America, David has begun to focus more time on writing materials designed to lead people into the kind of fulfilling life that God has for them. It was during the application of these materials at a lay retreat, and seeing peoples lives changed, that the idea of Live Free Ministries was born. From the original lay retreats, Live Free Ministries has branched out into radio, pastors retreats and support ministry, and a teaching newsletter.

Pursuing the call to the ministry, he graduated from Christ for the Nations and also took additional courses at Assemblies of God Theological Seminary. Besides his years as a pastor, David has had many opportunities to interact with people as a teacher in both public and Christian schools. With additional experiences as a Christian school principal and school board president, David feels the need to find solutions to the moral and spiritual crises in America that are ever more apparent today.

About Live Free Ministries

Birthed out of a heart to bring wholeness and hope to the body of Christ, Live Free Ministries is an inter-denominational Christian non-profit organization dependent upon the gifts of those with a vision for renewing God's people. Gifts to the organization are tax deductible.
Live Free Ministry Outreaches:

Real Questions Radio Program
Hosted by Live Free Ministries founder and President David A. Case and Dale Leach. Aired Monday's & Thursday's at 12:30CST KBBE 96.7 FM KNGL 1540 AM. The program addresses the tough issues facing Christians in today's society.
"Going Deeper" Retreats
Written and designed by Live Free Ministries President David A. Case.
Pastor's "Going Deeper" Retreats
Three day spiritual retreat to refresh, renew and bring victory in a deep walk with Christ. Focuses on spiritual authority, securing the harvest, and tools for a triumphant life. For pastors and their spouses.
Lay "Going Deeper" Retreats
Three day retreat to help the believer understand and overcome the hindrances of a Christian walk, resulting in a fuller experience of the love of God, and giving freedom to live as God desires.
Restoration Series Newsletter
A bi-monthly publication written by David A. Case. Mailed out free of charge to anyone in the USA. Brings insight and encouragement to those who desire to walk in a close relationship with God.

If you would like more information on Live Free Ministries, or to sign up to be on our mailing list and receive our Restoration Series Newsletter please fill out the information below and mail or call:
Live Free Ministries   (316)-241-8911
1064 14th Avenue, McPherson, KS 67460

Name_____Phone Number_____
Address_____
City_____State_____Zip_____

GOING DEEPER
BOOK ORDER FORM

If you would like more copies of <u>Going Deeper</u> by Author David A. Case, please fill out the form below and mail to:

Live Free Ministries
1064 14th Ave.
McPherson, KS 67460
(316)-241-8911
VISA & MASTERCARD orders are accepted over the phone.

All profits from the sale of this book go to support Live Free Ministries outreaches.

Please print clearly
NAME _____

ADDRESS _____

CITY _____STATE_____ZIP_____

PHONE NUMBER_____

PLEASE SEND ME _____ **COPIES OF** <u>**GOING DEEPER**</u>
Enclosed is my payment of **$9.50** per copy or
$7.50 per copy for orders of 10 or more.....................$_____
Enclosed for postage/handling
($2 – Orders up to $20; 10% of total for orders over $20)$_____
Enclosed is a support gift for the ministry.................$_____
Total Enclosed...$_____
Charge card

_____
Your name as it appears on your card

_____
Card number

_____   MasterCard_____   Visa_____
Expiration date